Solomon On Wealth

Solomon on Wealth

*Modern Financial Wisdom
From an Ancient King*

Stan Bullington, Ph.D.

Bully Pulpit Press
Starkville, Mississippi

Solomon on Wealth
Modern Financial Wisdom From an Ancient King
by Stan Bullington, Ph.D.

Published by
Bully Pulpit Press
P.O. Box 1504
Starkville, Mississippi 39760
www.bullypulpitpress.com

All rights reserved. No part of this book may be reproduced or transmitted in any form or by any means, electronic or mechanical, including photocopying, recording, or by any information storage and retrieval system, without written permission from the author, except for the inclusion of brief quotations in a review.

Copyright © 2008 by Stanley F. Bullington
ISBN-10: 0-9793322-2-2
ISBN-13: 978-0-9793322-2-7
Printed in the United States of America

All scripture quotations, unless otherwise indicated, are from the New King James Version®. Copyright © 1982 by Thomas Nelson, Inc. Used by permission. All rights reserved.

Publisher's Cataloging-in-Publication
(Provided by Quality Books, Inc.)

Bullington, Stan.
   Solomon on wealth : modern financial wisdom from an ancient king / Stan Bullington.
   p. cm.
   Includes bibliographical references and index.
   LCCN 2007902693
   ISBN-13: 978-0-9793322-2-7
   ISBN-10: 0-9793322-2-2
   1. Wealth--Biblical teaching. 2. Wealth--Religious aspects--Christianity. 3. Finance, Personal--Biblical teaching. 4. Finance, Personal--Religious aspects--Christianity. 5. Solomon, King of Israel--Miscellanea. I. Title.

BS680.W38B85 2007   241'.68
                       QBI07-600188

To Leanne, my virtuous wife, whose love and unfailing support have always helped me to reach higher

and

to my parents, Freed and Martha, whose godly lives have been such a powerful example to me and to so many others.

ACKNOWLEDGEMENTS

I am indebted most of all to my wife, Leanne. Her constant encouragement during the course of this project kept me going at several points when I wasn't sure I wanted to.

I received truly expert, yet kind, editorial assistance from my brother, Dr. Kimball Bullington, and my father-in-law, Bill Draffen. Additionally, Mr. Draffen's positive reactions to an early draft convinced me that I might be onto something – thank you! A number of others read drafts and made helpful and encouraging comments, including my parents, Freed and Martha Bullington, George and Becki Davis, and Boyd Sellers.

I am very grateful to Gary Henry, the author of *Diligently Seeking God*, for his advice on self-publishing, and to Dan Poynter, without whose fabulous book, *The Self-Publishing Manual*, I would have been quite lost. Peri Poloni-Gabriel of Knockout Design did a fabulous job with the cover design. My great friend, Dr. Bill Smyer, rendered invaluable technical assistance. My daughter, Suzanne, helped with web design work, and her siblings, Amy, Will, and Andrew, always thought what Dad was doing was pretty cool.

I am so thankful to many authors who have written about finances from a Biblical perspective – Ron Blue, the late Larry Burkett, Howard Dayton, and especially Dave Ramsey. Their work has helped so many gain a better understanding of God's plan for finances. Of course, I must thank our God and Father for giving us all that we have and making His wisdom known to us through men like King Solomon.

CONTENTS

	Preface	ix
1	We need Solomon's financial wisdom	11
2	Wealth is a blessing	19
3	Other blessings are more important than wealth	29
4	Wealth is a danger	39
5	Work diligently	55
6	Avoid debt	73
7	Help others	85

8	Trust God, not riches	93
9	A financial case study: the virtuous wife	101
10	Transform your life	111

Appendix 1 – Proverbs 30 and 31 on wealth	131
Appendix 2 – Financial books with a Biblical perspective	137
Appendix 3 – Getting started	143

Notes	147
General Index	151
Scripture Index	155
About the author	159

Preface

Christians are not immune to life's problems. As more and more people in our society struggle with financial difficulties (often of their own making), such problems become more widespread among God's people. We are in desperate need of a restoration of principles of financial management and behavior that were once common.

A few years ago, my wife and I became convinced that we needed to change our behavior in the area of finances. I would classify our approach to money in the early years of our marriage as being generally characterized by laziness. We did some things fairly well, and some things rather poorly. We began to read books. Many were excellent – especially those by Dave Ramsey, Ron Blue, and the late Larry Burkett. We particularly enjoyed and appreciated the authors who approached the study of finances from a Biblical perspective.

I decided to go back to the Source by looking directly at what God's Word has to say on finances, and to begin my study with the writings of Solomon. I knew this would be a rich study, but the more I looked into it, the more amazed I became. I did not recall from previous readings how specific and how timely some of Solomon's instructions on wealth are. As engineers are inclined to do, I began to classify and organize the things Solomon had written. When the classifying and organizing were fairly complete, I developed material for an adult Bible class I was teaching. I found that I wanted to take the study further, so I continued to refine the materials. This book is the product of that refinement. I sincerely hope that these thoughts will be as useful to others as they have been to me.

As you will note, I have included in the book the quotation of all the wealth-related passages from Proverbs and Ecclesiastes. In effect then, Solomon is my co-author. My point in saying that is this: *if you are tempted to skip over the scriptural passages in the book, please do not!* They are, obviously, the most important elements of what is here. I would hope that my comments will help illuminate Solomon's words to some extent, and to spur you to think about ways to implement Solomon's wisdom in your own life. Of course, there may be errors in some of my thinking. Hopefully, we all realize that there will be no errors in the words of the ancient king.

I should explain one other decision I have made that some readers may notice. Most scholars agree that the last two chapters of Proverbs were probably not written by Solomon. I have no reason to question their assessment, and have therefore decided to treat those chapters differently. The well known story of the virtuous wife in Proverbs 31:10-31 struck me as an outstanding case example of the implementation of Solomon's instructions on dealing with wealth, so I have dealt with it as such in chapter 9. The other wealth-related parts of Proverbs 30 and 31 are discussed as an appendix.

Chapter 1

We need Solomon's financial wisdom

Honor the Lord with your possessions, and with the firstfruits of all your increase.

Proverbs 3:9

An interviewer once asked golfing legend Gary Player what was the best advice anyone had ever given him. Player's reply had nothing to do with getting more distance on his tee shots, or being more consistent with his sand play or putting. The best advice he had ever received, he said, was to read the book of Proverbs.[1]

The Proverbs of King Solomon were written almost three thousand years ago. How relevant can they possibly be to our lives in the twenty-first century? This book is designed to show the relevance of the wisdom of Solomon to a key aspect of modern life – our finances. There is, indeed, a lot we can learn about wealth from Solomon. For example, we will learn what Solomon has to say about:

- financial priorities
- the benefits of saving
- how money can provide security
- the blessings of inheritances
- the (many) things that are better than wealth
- workaholics
- the dangers that can come with wealth
- how to use a financial windfall
- get-rich-quick schemes
- contentment
- abusing the poor
- the rewards of hard work
- the need for financial planning
- the need for careful asset management
- risk
- diversification
- laziness
- financial ethics and integrity
- the evils of indebtedness
- co-signing for a loan
- the best kind of investing
- the blessings of giving
- what the rich and poor have in common
- when wealth is worthless

Does this sound relevant to life in the twenty-first century? Of course it does. If you are interested in these

We Need Solomon's Financial Wisdom 13

issues, join me in a fascinating look at what Solomon has to say.

Solomon's name is synonymous (literally) with wisdom. We are told (in I Kings 4:29-34) of how God blessed Solomon with "wisdom and exceedingly great understanding"[2] such that he was said to be "wiser than all men." He was also blessed with great wealth (see I Kings 10:14-29). In fact, his income in gold might be estimated to have been equivalent to well over $500,000,000 per year![3]

Now think with me. Who do you want to listen to for financial advice? Would you be more inclined to listen to a poor person or a wealthy person? That's an easy one. Would you rather listen to a wise wealthy person or a foolish wealthy person? Yes, there are some foolish wealthy people. In fact, Solomon talks about them. I'm going to use the wise wealthy financial advisor.

Solomon, as we will see, had much to say about financial matters. Fortunately for us, Solomon was a prolific writer, and left a record of his financial (and other) wisdom in the books of Proverbs and Ecclesiastes. Of course, Bible believers know that we can trust Solomon's financial advice even further because God was directing his thoughts. In fact, the entire Bible is filled with God's financial wisdom. In fact, it has been estimated that the Bible contains more than 2,350 verses on money and possessions, as compared to just over 500 verses on prayer and just under 500 verses on faith.[4] You see, God knew that people would always struggle with finances. Yet God does not want His children to be consumed with the cares and worries of this world. He left us a way to avoid the constant financial struggles and worries that so many around us contend with. How terribly sad it is that those who are supposed to be His children often ignore His plan for financial peace and security!

The Problem in Our World

Our world, and especially the U.S., could use a heavy dose of wisdom from Solomon on the world of work and money. Consider the following facts regarding money in our society:

- Around 70% of Americans live from paycheck to paycheck.[5]
- 1.65 million personal bankruptcies were filed in the U.S. in 2003.[6]
- The average credit card debt of U.S. households with at least one card rose from $2,966 in 1990 to $9,205 in 2003 – a 310% increase.[7]
- About 70% of divorcing couples attribute their marriage breakdown primarily to arguments over money.[8]
- 32% of corporate human resource executives surveyed cited lost productivity due to financial stress as the most pressing overlooked issue in the workplace.[9]
- The average credit card balance for senior citizens increased by 89 percent between 1992 and 2001.[10]
- A U.S. national research study reported that adolescents listed financial problems among the top ten sources of stress in their lives.[11]

- Surveys report that charitable giving by Christians has declined from about 4% of income to about 2% in the last forty years.[12]

Something is clearly wrong here. Things are bad, and they are quickly getting worse. Furthermore, note that the evidence indicates that money problems affect virtually every segment of society, including those who claim to be Christians.

There are a number of rather obvious causes for the symptoms listed above. Materialism is rampant in our culture. It was rampant in Solomon's culture, too. Some of us are lazy – either in our work, or in our money management, or both. Solomon saw the same problems. Many people today are driven by short-term thinking, just as many were in Solomon's day. Sadly, Christians suffer from all of these problems, and the situation among believers also appears to be worsening (as evidenced by the above statistic on declining charitable giving, for instance). If God's people behave like those around them and fall into the trap of materialism, or even just financial laziness, they will probably find themselves in trouble with debt, marital difficulties, money stress, or the other problems that financial difficulties bring. When this happens, how likely is it that we will be able to honor the Lord with our possessions, and with the *firstfruits* of all our increase (see Proverbs 3:9)?

It is long past time for us to become familiar with God's plan for our finances, *and to implement it in our lives* if we have not already done so. Regarding financial matters, as well as all others, we need to ask ourselves "what does God's word tell me about this?"

Solomon's Financial Advice

In his fabulous little book, *Heart, Soul, and Money*, Craig L. Blomberg presents a brief summary of what the Bible has to say about the Christian and his finances. Blomberg concludes that the bulk of Biblical teaching on finances is captured in the following five points:

- Material possessions are a gift from God meant for His people to enjoy and share.
- Material possessions are also one of the primary means of turning hearts away from God.
- The mature Christian should be a good steward of God's gifts.
- Both extreme wealth and extreme poverty are intolerable.
- The way we treat material things is an indication of our spiritual condition.[13]

In this book, we will undertake a narrower, but more detailed, study than Blomberg's, focusing on Solomon's financial wisdom. I carefully read the books of Proverbs and Ecclesiastes (and the two recorded Psalms attributed to Solomon) in order to identify all of the passages dealing with wealth. I then summarized the thoughts in each passage, and grouped passages with similar thoughts. The following seven key ideas emerged from this study:

- Wealth is a blessing.
- Other blessings are more important than wealth.

- Wealth is a danger.
- Work diligently.
- Avoid debt.
- Help others.
- Trust God, not riches.

We should make some observations regarding these key thoughts before we examine each one in detail in the chapters that follow. First, you can easily note the similarities between this list, which is based on Solomon's writing, and Blomberg's list, which is based on all the Biblical writers. This is not surprising, since we would expect Solomon's message to be in agreement with the other inspired authors. Second, note that the first three ideas listed above describe aspects or characteristics of wealth that we need to understand. Learning more about how God views wealth should help us transform our attitudes toward it, which should lead to changes in our financial behavior. The last four ideas listed above present specific actions that we ought to take relating to wealth.

The instructions that Solomon presents should serve as the foundation of every Christian's financial planning and behavior. Although summarizing Solomon's wisdom with such a simple list is extremely valuable, the beauty of this study is in the details. The next seven chapters will examine each of these key ideas in turn by looking at everything that Solomon says about each idea, and by thinking about how the ideas apply to us. In chapter nine, we will look at the story of the virtuous wife (Proverbs 31:10-31), as a case study of one who follows God's financial plan. We will conclude in chapter ten with some thoughts on how we

18 Solomon on Wealth

can make Solomon's instructions work in our lives today, so that we can be as effective as possible in our service to God.

Chapter 2

Wealth is a blessing

*The blessing of the Lord makes one rich,
and He adds no sorrow with it.*

Proverbs 10:22

The idea that poverty is somehow more spiritual or holy than wealth seems to be a fairly common belief among religious people. Others seem to feel that wealth is something that the child of God should avoid. Although it is easy to understand how people could have these misconceptions, a careful study of all that the Scriptures have to say about wealth and poverty make it clear that such thoughts are not scriptural. In his book, *Financial Peace Revisited*, financial counselor Dave Ramsey makes the point that money is amoral – that money itself is neither good nor bad.[1] Like other blessings, money can be used correctly (i.e., according to God's plan), or incorrectly.

It is obvious, as we shall soon see, that there are many warnings about the dangers of wealth. However, there are also many passages that clearly teach that wealth is a blessing from God that He wishes His people to use in His service. In this chapter, we will look at twenty passages where Solomon discusses wealth as a blessing. Solomon will tell us that God promises to bless people who follow His plan, that wealth is a blessing in several different ways, and that God gives us directions on how to use our wealth in His service.

God Blesses Those Who are Righteous and Wise

Those who follow God's plan of salvation will be saved. Those who follow God's plan for marriage will be good husbands and wives. Those who follow God's plan for parenting will be good parents. God's plan is always the best plan – in every realm of life! If God has given us instructions about how to deal with financial matters and about the proper role of wealth in the life of the Christian – and He has – then we can have absolute confidence (i.e., trust) that His plan for finances is a good one. Let's see what God says about the blessing of wealth for those who are willing to put their complete trust in God in this matter, and to follow His plan.

Wealth is a Blessing

Honor the Lord with your possessions, and with the firstfruits of all your increase; so your barns will be filled with plenty, and your vats will overflow with new wine.

Proverbs 3:9-10

By humility and fear of the Lord are riches and honor and life.

Proverbs 22:4

Treasures of wickedness profit nothing, but righteousness delivers from death. The Lord will not allow the righteous soul to famish, but He casts away the desire of the wicked.

Proverbs 10:2-3

In the house of the righteous, there is much treasure, but in the revenue of the wicked is trouble.

Proverbs 15:6

There is desirable treasure, and oil in the dwelling of the wise, but a foolish man squanders it.

Proverbs 21:20

Through wisdom a house is built, and by understanding it is established; by knowledge the rooms are filled with all precious and pleasant riches.

Proverbs 24:3-4

The crown of the wise is their riches, but the foolishness of fools is folly.

Proverbs 14:24

22   Solomon on Wealth

Wealth is like many other blessings from God – it can be abused and lead to sin, as we will see in a later chapter. However, Solomon tells us that God wants those who follow Him to enjoy material blessings. This is not to say that God promises material wealth to all His people. This is a rather popular false doctrine that seems to be motivated largely by greed on the part of those who teach it. The above passages show us that, in general, those who follow God will be blessed in every way, including financially.

God asks us to honor Him with the firstfruits (i.e., the first and best) of all that we have. Imagine a Jewish farmer in Solomon's time. The farmer worked hard preparing his fields, sowing his seed, waiting for the crops to grow, and then, finally, the first of his harvest arrived. This was the first opportunity for the farmer to gain materially from all of his labor, yet God asked him to give his firstfruits as an offering. There was no way for the farmer to know whether or not pests or weather might destroy most or all of the rest of his crop, leaving him financially ruined. It showed great trust and faith in God for the farmer to make this sacrifice! This is the attitude God expects from us, also. Our trust is to be in God, rather than in our own possessions or skill. If we have this kind of trust, God is promising to bless us. Do we believe Him enough to follow His plan?

Notice the results of trusting God in this respect, as indicated in these verses – barns filled with plenty, vats overflowing with new wine, riches, much treasure, desirable treasure and oil, all precious and pleasant riches. These blessings are gifts from God – gifts for the righteous. Wealth is not, in and of itself, an indication of materialism or greed or lack of spirituality. For those who follow God's plan, wealth will often result. We need to make sure we have the proper attitude toward it, and know how to use it in the way God directs.

Proverbs 21:20 presents a contrast between the way the wise and foolish handle their wealth. The wise man is said to have desirable treasure and oil. God has provided these blessings, and the wise man has managed them well, so that they are available later when needed. On the other hand, the foolish man is one who did possess wealth, but chose to squander it. This verse shows the benefits of saving for the future, as opposed to wasting wealth. We need to think about what kind of stewards we have been. Have we done well in managing the material blessings God has given us, or have we foolishly let them slip away?

Wealth as a Blessing

Once we realize that wealth is a blessing from God, and is meant to be used in His service, we ought to be able to see the importance of properly using this blessing. There is no reason to feel guilty if we are blessed materially, just as we should not feel guilty if we are blessed in any other way. The proper response to any blessing is thankfulness, humility, and determination to fulfill the responsibilities that come to those who are blessed. Consider the verses that follow.

Solomon on Wealth

The blessing of the Lord makes one rich, and He adds no sorrow with it.

Proverbs 10:22

Better is the one who is slighted but has a servant, than he who honors himself but lacks bread.

Proverbs 12:9

A present is a precious stone in the eyes of its possessor; wherever he turns, he prospers.

Proverbs 17:8

The rich man's wealth is his strong city; the destruction of the poor is their poverty.

Proverbs 10:15

For wisdom is a defense as money is a defense, but the excellence of knowledge is that wisdom gives life to those who have it.

Ecclesiastes 7:12

The ransom of a man's life is his riches, but the poor does not hear rebuke.

Proverbs 13:8

Wealth can do many things for the servant of God. As Proverbs 10:22 clearly shows us, riches that come as a blessing from the Lord – as opposed to wealth gained through illicit means – bring no sorrow with them. There is absolutely no cause for the wealthy righteous person to feel guilty about these blessings! On the contrary, they should rejoice in them and use them as God directs. As we see here, money serves as a defense – a strong city – protecting the blessed one from many of the cares that threaten to overwhelm those who struggle financially. We have here a picture of financial security for those who understand how to use God's blessings properly. Solomon will have much more to say about how this can be done.

Good Ways to Use Wealth

Although we did not always note it, the passages in the previous two sections have implied several proper uses for wealth. These include (1) honoring the Lord with the firstfruits of our increase, (2) providing for needed sustenance, and (3) providing financial security and protection. There are a number of passages where Solomon deals more explicitly with the proper use of wealth. Consider the seven passages that follow.

> A good man leaves an inheritance to his children's children, but the wealth of the sinner is stored up for the righteous.
> Proverbs 13:22

> The righteous eats to the satisfying of the soul, but the stomach of the wicked shall be in want.
> Proverbs 13:25

Nothing is better for a man than that he should eat and drink, and that his soul should enjoy good in his labor. This also, I saw, was from the hand of God.
Ecclesiastes 2:24

I know that nothing is better for them than to rejoice, and to do good in their lives, and also that every man should eat and drink and enjoy the good of all his labor – it is the gift of God.
Ecclesiastes 3:12-13

Here is what I have seen: It is good and fitting for one to eat and drink, and to enjoy the good of all his labor in which he toils under the sun all the days of his life which God gives him; for it is his heritage. As for every man to whom God has given riches and wealth, and given him power to eat of it, to receive his heritage and rejoice in his labor – this is the gift of God. For he will not dwell unduly on the days of his life, because God keeps him busy with the joy of his heart.
Ecclesiastes 5:18-20

So I commended enjoyment, because a man has nothing better under the sun than to eat, drink, and be merry; for this will remain with him in his labor all the days of his life which God gives him under the sun.
Ecclesiastes 8:15

Go, eat your bread with joy, and drink your wine with a merry heart, for God has already accepted your works. Let your garments always be white, and let your head lack no oil. Live joyfully with the wife whom you love all the days of your vain life which He has given you under the sun, all your days of vanity; for that is your portion in life, and in the labor which you perform under the sun.
Ecclesiastes 9:7-9

Among the many false ideas that some religious people have about wealth is the notion that God's people should have no concern for material things, and should therefore make no financial plans for the future, but simply trust in God to take care of their financial future for them. This is not God's plan! Jesus Himself spoke approvingly of financial planning (see Luke 14:28-30). The apostle Paul reproved some of the Thessalonians for failing to work due to their mistaken belief that Christ's second coming was imminent (see II Thessalonians 3:10-12). Here in Proverbs 13:22, we see that a good man has the foresight to provide for his family's financial future by leaving an inheritance for his grandchildren. Working (and saving) to provide for one's family is a divinely approved use of wealth.

The rest of these passages point out that it is fitting for one to enjoy the benefits of his or her own hard work. Pay special attention to Ecclesiastes 5:19, which explicitly refers to a man's riches and wealth as a gift from God, and encourages the use of a portion of those gifts for one's own enjoyment and pleasure.

Points to Remember

Wealth is a blessing from God, which He encourages us to use in a number of ways, including (1) to honor God with the firstfruits, (2) to provide needed sustenance, (3) to provide financial security and protection, (4) to provide for one's family, including through inheritances, and (5) to enjoy. In a later chapter, we will look at several passages that discuss another approved use for wealth, namely, (6) to share it with others. Clearly, God wants us to view wealth as a valuable blessing. However, as we will see in the next two chapters, wealth is less important than many other blessings and can, in fact, be a great danger for those who have improper attitudes toward wealth, or who fail to use it as God directs.

Chapter 3

Other blessings are more important than wealth

Better is a little with righteousness, than vast revenues without justice.

Proverbs 16:8

We have seen that wealth is a blessing for the people of God. Wealth can help us do many useful things in service to God. We must be careful, however, not to overemphasize the importance of wealth. Solomon makes some direct comparisons between wealth and other blessings in order to help us understand the proper role of wealth in the Christian's life so that we will never let the pursuit and use of wealth become too important to us. There are, in fact, many blessings from God that are of far greater value than wealth. Solomon identifies several, as we will see in this chapter. Jesus also plainly teaches us that our most valuable possession – our soul – is infinitely more important than material wealth. (See Matthew 16:26).

Wisdom is Better than Wealth

The key word in the book of Proverbs is "wisdom." Solomon indicates immediately (Proverbs 1:1-7) that his purpose in writing is to impart wisdom to those who are willing to hear. It is not surprising, then, that Solomon would directly contrast wealth with wisdom. The following passages present this contrast.

> How much better to get wisdom than gold! And to get understanding is to be chosen rather than silver.
>
> **Proverbs 16:16**

> Happy is the man who finds wisdom, and the man who gains understanding; for her proceeds are better than the profits of silver, and her gain than fine gold. She is more precious than rubies, and all the things you may desire cannot compare with her. Length of days is in her right hand, in her left hand riches and honor. Her ways are ways of pleasantness, and all her paths are peace. She is a tree of life to those who take hold of her, and happy are all who retain her.
>
> **Proverbs 3:13-18**

Other Blessings are More Important than Wealth

Receive my instruction, and not silver, and knowledge rather than choice gold; for wisdom is better than rubies, and all the things one may desire cannot be compared with her. I, wisdom, dwell with prudence, and find out knowledge and discretion. The fear of the Lord is to hate evil; pride and arrogance and the evil way and the perverse mouth I hate. Counsel is mine, and sound wisdom; I am understanding. I have strength. By me kings reign, and rulers decree justice. By me princes rule, and nobles, all the judges of the earth. I love those who love me, and those who seek me diligently will find me. Riches and honor are with me, enduring riches and righteousness. My fruit is better than gold, yes, than fine gold, and my revenue than choice silver. I traverse the way of righteousness, in the midst of the paths of justice, that I may cause those who love me to inherit wealth, that I may fill their treasuries.

Proverbs 8:10-21

Whoever loves wisdom makes his father rejoice, but a companion of harlots wastes his wealth.

Proverbs 29:3

Poverty and shame will come to him who disdains correction, but he who regards a rebuke will be honored.

Proverbs 13:18

These passages not only tell us that wisdom is better than riches, but they also give us some insight into why this is true. True wisdom leads one to fear the Lord (see Proverbs 8:12-14). Those who fear the Lord enjoy many blessings, including riches, length of days, honor, a pleasant and peaceful life, justice, and righteousness. This does not mean that righteous people do not die young or suffer hardships. They sometimes do. It was Solomon who said that "time and chance happen to them all" (Ecclesiastes 9:11) and "all things come alike to all" (Ecclesiastes 9:2). But Solomon is telling us that God's plan for living is the best plan. If we will learn wisdom from God, we will ultimately receive God's salvation. Furthermore, even in this life, we will generally enjoy more blessings by following God's plan than will those who live after their own wisdom. This includes the area of finances – God's way is best!

So why then is wisdom better than wealth? Quite simply, wisdom will help one live in God's way, which will result in blessings of all kinds, including financial blessings. We might say that wisdom is a cause, while wealth is just one of its effects, and certainly not its most important effect.

Solomon's words in Proverbs 29:3 and Proverbs 13:18 remind us of the Lord's parable of the prodigal son (Luke 15:11-32). Like many foolish people in our day, the prodigal son believed in living for the moment. He could not wait for the appropriate time to receive his inheritance, but demanded it *now!* Then, when he had the inheritance, he failed to use it wisely, but wasted it (with harlots, according to his older brother). His failure to heed wise counsel led to his poverty and shame. Imagine how differently things would have worked out for him if he had read and followed Solomon's instructions on wealth. Yet it is easy for us to look around us today and see countless people living exactly like this foolish son lived. The wisdom is still there, teaching us today, if we are only willing to learn!

Other Blessings are More Important than Wealth

A Righteous Life is Better than Wealth

There are ungodly people who seem to enjoy life, and who certainly have great material wealth. However, there are many ungodly wealthy people whose lives are full of unhappiness. Solomon wants us to know that the poor, but righteous, individual is really much better off than the ungodly person with great wealth. The wise know that wealth is fleeting and that contentment is one of God's "secrets" for happiness (see I Timothy 6:6-10). People need God – not great wealth – in order to enjoy life to its fullest!

Better is a little with righteousness, than vast revenues without justice.
Proverbs 16:8

Better is the poor who walks in his integrity than one perverse in his ways, though he be rich.
Proverbs 28:6

A good name is to be chosen rather than great riches, loving favor rather than silver and gold.
Proverbs 22:1

A gracious woman retains honor, but ruthless men retain riches.
Proverbs 11:16

In Proverbs 16:8, Solomon refers to those who have "vast revenues without justice." The Bible (particularly the Old Testament prophets) repeatedly condemns those who oppress the poor. (See, for example, Isaiah 3:13-15; Micah 2:1-2; Zechariah 7:9-10). God knew that the greedy rich would be tempted to trample on the poor in their search for more wealth. Christians can fall into the same trap! We will deal with this thought more completely in the following chapter, but it won't hurt to make the point here, as well. Treating others unjustly in order to take financial advantage of them is just one of the many temptations and snares into which the greedy may fall (see I Timothy 6:9-10). If we are committed to living righteously before God, and justly to others, we will be able to avoid this trap, even if we are among the wealthy. However, if you are wealthy and are tempted in this way, it would be a good idea to start looking for ways to give up your wealth, rather than to let your wealth cost you your soul. Jesus Himself gave this advice in such a situation (Matthew 19:16-22).

The last three passages above deal with what we might call "reputation." What is a good reputation worth? Solomon says that it is worth more than great wealth. Another way to think about this question is to consider how difficult it is to acquire a good reputation once it has been lost or damaged. How much effort – "cost," we might say – must be expended to get a good name once it has been lost through some sin? Many of us have known people who have developed a reputation as a liar, for example. How hard is it for that person to acquire a reputation as one who is trustworthy? Sadly, in some cases, such a history may never be

Other Blessings are More Important than Wealth

erased completely from the minds of others. Children of God may face temptations in their business or workplace to be dishonest in order to "get ahead." Don't give in! One slip-up may be enough to damage a reputation irreparably. No amount of financial gain is worth this!

Honesty really is the best policy, even though it might sometimes come at a high price. There may be sales that are lost or promotions that are denied as a direct result of our being honest. So be it! If we lose a chance at wealth that could have been obtained by risking our reputation, we have made the best choice, according to Solomon.

But there is another side to this story, also. Think about business people you know who are trying to serve God and follow His plan in all things. These people, no doubt, are known for their integrity and good reputation. Do such people tend to be successful in their business dealings? Typically, the answer is yes. People love to do business with those who are completely trustworthy. So, even though there may be a short-term cost associated with following God's instructions in some business situations, once again we see that God's plan is the best way. This is always true in the long-term (i.e., eternally), but is most often true in this earthly life, as well.

A Peaceful Life is Better than Wealth

Some wealthy people are happy. Some are miserable. Wealth does not necessarily bring happiness, nor does it necessarily bring misery. Our attitude toward

Solomon on Wealth

material things, and our ability to understand how to use them, will generally determine whether our material possessions help us enjoy life as God intended, or whether they pull us away from God into a selfish existence, which tends to be a miserable one. Solomon had a lot to say about this, as we see below.

> Better is a little with the fear of the Lord, than great treasure with trouble. Better is a dinner of herbs where love is, than a fatted calf with hatred.
>
> Proverbs 15:16-17

> Better is a dry morsel with quietness, than a house full of feasting with strife.
>
> Proverbs 17:1

> Better to dwell in a corner of a housetop, than in a house shared with a contentious woman.
>
> Proverbs 21:9

> Better a handful with quietness than both hands full, together with toil and grasping for the wind.
>
> Ecclesiastes 4:6

> There is one alone, without companion: he has neither son nor brother. Yet there is no end to all his labors, nor is his eye satisfied with riches. But he never asks, "For whom do I toil and deprive myself of good?" This also is vanity and a grave misfortune.
>
> Ecclesiastes 4:8

Other Blessings are More Important than Wealth

Wealth that is accompanied by hatred, strife, and contention leads to an unfulfilled, miserable life. As we have seen, material possessions are gifts from God, and are meant to bring pleasure. It is ironic, then, that dedicating one's life to the pursuit of material gain tends to lead ultimately to unhappiness and frustration. Solomon makes this very plain. Look again at Ecclesiastes 4:6 above. A peaceful life with very little of this world's goods is greatly preferred to a life devoted to the pursuit of "stuff." Stuff doesn't last. Stuff promises happiness, but generally fails to deliver as advertised. To look for happiness through material possessions is just like trying to grasp the wind.

Why do so many people – even those who would call themselves Christians – live this way? The temptation is strong. We see worldly people who make wealth their goal, and who appear to be having so much fun. In many cases, the situation is not as it appears to be – the private lives of these rich people may be empty and filled with despair. But there are definitely times when these people really *are* having a lot of fun! Even so, we should realize, as Moses did, that these pleasures are fleeting (see Hebrews 11:24-26). They will not be around long enough to warrant giving our lives up to obtain them. God's way is best!

The last of the passages above, Ecclesiastes 4:8, presents a classic picture of what we would call a workaholic. This man is working for no one but himself; he has no one with whom to share the fruits of his labor. Furthermore, he does not even take the time to enjoy what he has gained. The man is driven by the desire to accumulate more. Wealth, and the struggle to obtain it, has become his god. Solomon sees this as "vanity and a grave misfortune." Imagine how much good many of these people could have accomplished if they had put this kind of energy into serving God and helping their fellow man. Think of the fulfillment of seeing their efforts bless others. How sad that they would be so misguided! What a grave misfortune!

Points to Remember

Wealth should be a wonderful blessing from God, but it is not among the most important blessings for His dedicated servants. It cannot compare with wisdom, which will help us see the right path to take in all aspects of our lives, including our finances. No amount of wealth is worth the sacrifice of our integrity and reputation. Wealth achieved through dishonest dealings is no bargain. Finally, those who devote all their energies to the pursuit of material possessions miss the point of life, and are likely to be sorely disappointed, even in the here and now. Solomon speaks so clearly toward those who suffer from workaholism. They are unlikely to succeed in any meaningful sense, and they are unlikely to obtain any degree of real fulfillment.

Hopefully, the passages we have looked at in this chapter will help us to better understand the nature of wealth. God wants His people to be good stewards of their blessings – to honor Him with their possessions, to see their physical needs met, to enjoy these blessings, and to share them with others. If we use wealth correctly, we will be blessed. If we make wealth our goal, we will certainly be disappointed.

Chapter 4

Wealth is a danger

A faithful man will abound with blessings, but he who hastens to be rich will not go unpunished.

Proverbs 28:20

We have seen that wealth is a blessing from God, and is meant to be used in His service. We have also seen that wealth is certainly not the greatest of the blessings that God gives us. In this chapter, we will look at what Solomon has to say about the negative side of wealth. Solomon warns us that wealth can be a danger to us. Materialism is rampant in our society. Christians are not immune from this weakness, and often find themselves caught up in the pursuit of wealth. In attempting to avoid this mistake, some of God's people have gone to the other extreme and have tended to view wealth as an evil. Understanding the Biblical view of wealth will help us keep our priorities straight, and will help us avoid the dangers that Solomon warns us about.

Do Not Lose Sight of Proper Priorities

Satan uses the lust of the flesh, the lust of the eyes, and the pride of life to tempt us to sin (I John 2:15-17). The desire for material wealth is a strong drive. If we ever lose sight of the proper role of wealth in our lives, it is just a short step from there to the point where we become driven by a selfish desire for material things.

Contrary to popular opinion, the Bible does *not* say that "money is the root of all evil." What it clearly *does* say is that "the *love* of money is a root of all kinds of evil" (I Timothy 6:10). The servant of God must always be on guard against developing a love for material possessions. In Luke 16:13, Jesus said it this way: "No servant can serve two masters; for either he will hate the one and love the other, or else he will be loyal to the one and despise the other. You cannot serve God and mammon" [literally, wealth]. Simply put, if you love riches, you do not love God! Solomon deals at length with this issue of keeping wealth in perspective. Consider the six passages below.

> Do not overwork to be rich; because of your own understanding, cease! Will you set your eyes on that which is not? For riches certainly make themselves wings; they fly away like an eagle toward heaven.
>
> **Proverbs 23:4-5**

Wealth is a Danger

It is vain for you to rise up early, to sit up late, to eat the bread of sorrows; for so He gives His beloved sleep.

Psalm 127:2

A faithful man will abound with blessings, but he who hastens to be rich will not go unpunished.

Proverbs 28:20

A man with an evil eye hastens after riches, and does not consider that poverty will come upon him.

Proverbs 28:22

If you see the oppression of the poor, and the violent perversion of justice and righteousness in a province, do not marvel at the matter; for high official watches over high official, and higher officials are over them. Moreover the profit of the land is for all; even the king is served from the field. He who loves silver will not be satisfied with silver; nor he who loves abundance, with increase. This also is vanity. When goods increase, they increase who eat them; so what profit have the owners except to see them with their eyes? The sleep of a laboring man is sweet, whether he eats little or much; but the abundance of the rich will not permit him to sleep. There is a severe evil which I have seen under the sun: riches kept for their owner to his hurt. But those riches perish through misfortune; when he begets a son, there is nothing in his hand. As he came from his mother's womb, naked shall he return, to go as he came; and he shall take nothing from his labor which he may carry away in his hand. And this also is a severe evil – just exactly as he came, so shall he go. And what profit has he who has labored for the wind? All his days he also eats in darkness, and he has much sorrow and sickness and anger. Here is what I have seen: It is good and fitting for one to eat and drink, and to enjoy the good of all his labor in which he toils under the sun all the days of his life which God gives him; for it is his heritage.

Ecclesiastes 5:8-17

> There is an evil which I have seen under the sun, and it is common among men: A man to whom God has given riches and wealth and honor, so that he lacks nothing for himself of all he desires; yet God does not give him power to eat of it, but a foreigner consumes it. This is vanity, and it is an evil affliction. If a man begets a hundred children and lives many years, so that the days of his years are many, but his soul is not satisfied with goodness, or indeed he has no burial, I say that a stillborn child is better than he – for it comes in vanity and departs in darkness, and its name is covered with darkness. Though it has not seen the sun or known anything, this has more rest than that man, even if he lives a thousand years twice – but has not seen goodness. Do not all go to one place? All the labor of man is for his mouth, and yet the soul is not satisfied. For what more has the wise man than the fool? What does the poor man have, who knows how to walk before the living? Better is the sight of the eyes than the wandering of desire. This also is vanity and grasping for the wind.
>
> Ecclesiastes 6:1-9

Workaholism is a fairly modern word, but it is certainly not a modern phenomenon. Solomon addresses it directly here in Proverbs 23:4-5 and Psalm 127:2 (one of the few recorded Psalms of Solomon). A contemporary paraphrase of these verses might go something like this: "Don't work all the time just to accumulate stuff. Use your head! Stop it! Why spend all your time and energy chasing after things that don't last?" How many people do we see around us who are definitely *not* using their heads in this regard? People work incredibly long hours just to buy things that they don't even have enough time to enjoy. Many people do this purely out of pride, so that they can maintain a standard of living that will impress their neighbors or relatives. Not only does this workaholism not bring them fulfillment and satisfaction, but think of the other negative consequences – neglected children, neglected spouses, high levels of stress, health problems, and on and on. Why do people do this? As Solomon says here, *there is no good reason for it!*

It's not too surprising to find worldly people caught in this trap of pursuing things that don't matter. Unfortunately, Christians often fall into the trap, as well. We may feel that we can't "keep up" at work without putting in the long hours. We may work in environments where everyone else is putting in long hours. We may just simply be interested in acquiring more stuff! Whatever our reasons, or rationalizations, may be for overworking (Solomon's word), when it comes right down to it, we just aren't using our heads! When God's people overwork in their pursuit of material possessions, pride, status, or any other worldly goal, Satan wins.

The next two passages – Proverbs 28:20 and 28:22 – both refer to those who "hasten to be rich." People who make wealth their primary goal often become so intent on obtaining it that they fail to be concerned about what they might have to do, or who might be hurt in their struggle. The contrast in verse 20 is interesting. The faithful man will be blessed. The one who rushes headlong in a pursuit for wealth will be punished. According to verse 22, part of that punishment will be poverty. This brings to mind some of the corporate executives of our day who amass great wealth at the expense of their companies' employees and stockholders, only to end up disgraced, impoverished, and imprisoned. It also reminds us of the lottery winners who quickly squander their newfound "easy money." In the following chapter, we will examine God's plan for acquiring wealth. We will see that it depends on hard work. God's plan works! "Get rich quick" schemes generally don't work at all. Even in the odd cases where they do appear to work, they are still not smart. If it looks like a quick way to wealth, beware! Remember Solomon's clear warnings to those who would hasten to be rich.

The passages in Ecclesiastes 5 and 6 are so filled with financial wisdom that they deserve much more detailed study than we can give them here. In Ecclesiastes 5:8, Solomon says that "high official watches over high official, and higher officials are over them." Think about what this is saying to those who spend their lives working to move up the organizational ladder. No matter how high you go, you still have bosses! There are very few circumstances where you are not answerable to someone. Therefore, making power and position your goal is generally a futile struggle.

In 5:10, Solomon points out that wealth alone does not satisfy. If the goal is to accumulate more, this is a lust that can never be fully realized. How much is enough for a person who is driven to get more? Solomon concludes that such a life is vanity.

Even when a person is successful in accumulating wealth, their success often results in the attraction of others ("friends") who would like "a piece of the action." For this reason, and several others, wealth is a difficult thing to hang on to. The struggle for wealth, and even the wealth itself, also often brings problems and worries that take away the joy that should accompany God's blessings (Ecclesiastes 5:12). Misfortune can also cause the loss of wealth (5:13). The overall picture of these verses in chapter 5 is that wealth is not a good goal for your life. It is too easily lost, and it brings with it too much worry and trouble. How much better is it to live for God, to follow His plan for our finances, to enjoy the blessings He gives, and to use them as He directs! Just think of all the people in our world today whose lives could be so much richer and more enjoyable if they would read and heed Solomon's wisdom as recorded here.

The passage that perhaps best summarizes Solomon's thoughts here is Ecclesiastes 6:6, when he says, "Do not all go to one place?" We are all going to die – the rich and the poor. We had better live our lives in recognition of that fact, rather than living them in pursuit of these material things that will all be destroyed. We must not lose sight of the proper priorities for our lives!

Wealth Often Leads to Pride

One of the ugliest words in all of Scripture is "pride." There is no favorable use of this word throughout the Bible. Solomon had much to say about the evils of pride – most famously in Proverbs 16:18, which says that "pride goes before destruction, and a haughty spirit before a fall," and in Proverbs 6:16-17, where "a proud look" is listed first among seven things that the Lord hates.

Those who are rich are particularly susceptible to pride. Since pride has no place in the life of a Christian, those Christians who are wealthy must be on guard against it. Consider the following verses in this regard.

> The rich man is wise in his own eyes. But the poor who has understanding searches him out.
>
> **Proverbs 28:11**
>
> The poor man uses entreaties, but the rich answers roughly.
>
> **Proverbs 18:23**
>
> A feast is made for laughter, and wine makes merry; but money answers everything.
>
> **Ecclesiastes 10:19**

The rich person who is proud often feels as if he has all the answers. His success in the financial arena leads him to believe that he can deal with anything. Like the Old Testament Israelites who turned their hearts away from God when their armies were strong, the rich man may put so much stock in his wealth that he forgets about his need for God. He may feel as if his money "answers everything" (Ecclesiastes 10:19) – in other words, he feels that his money can provide for every need that he has. Solomon says in Proverbs 28:11 that the poor man who has understanding knows much more than this haughty rich man.

Poor people may find it easy to have humility. Their financial circumstances may serve to help keep them humble. Therefore, when they need something, they are much more likely to ask for it with an attitude of humility. The rich, on the other hand, are more likely to be accustomed to having things done their way. This can – but does not have to – lead to the rich treating others with condescension. God's people, no matter what their financial circumstances may be, need to be humble and kind in their dealings with others. To the degree that riches make this difficult for the rich, they represent a danger to our spiritual well being.

Beware of the Dangers of Greed

Wealth can act much like a narcotic – the more of it some people get, the more of it they want, and the harder it is for them to think of anything else. Solomon warns repeatedly against becoming greedy. Consider the passages below.

He who is greedy for gain troubles his own house, but he who hates bribes will live.
Proverbs 15:27

My son, if sinners entice you, do not consent. If they say, "Come with us, let us lie in wait to shed blood; let us lurk secretly for the innocent without cause; let us swallow them alive like Sheol, and whole, like those who go down to the Pit; we shall find all kinds of precious possessions, we shall fill our houses with spoil; cast in your lot among us, let us all have one purse" – My son, do not walk in the way with them, keep your feet from their path; for their feet run to evil, and they make haste to shed blood. Surely, in vain the net is spread in the sight of any bird; but they lie in wait for their own blood, they lurk secretly for their own lives. So are the ways of everyone who is greedy for gain; it takes away the life of its owners.

Proverbs 1:10-19

The poor man is hated even by his own neighbor, but the rich has many friends.

Proverbs 14:20

Wealth makes many friends, but the poor is separated from his friend.

Proverbs 19:4

Many entreat the favor of the nobility, and every man is a friend to one who gives gifts. All the brothers of the poor hate him; how much more do his friends go far from him! He may pursue them with words, yet they abandon him.

Proverbs 19:6-7

Luxury is not fitting for a fool, much less for a servant to rule over princes.

Proverbs 19:10

Have you found honey? Eat only as much as you need, lest you be filled with it and vomit.

Proverbs 25:16

Those who are greedy, Solomon says, bring troubles upon their own house. Think of the families of those found guilty of "white-collar crime." How many innocent spouses, children, and other family members have paid dearly for the greed-driven mistakes of their loved ones? It's not worth it! God's plan calls for those in positions of power and influence to remain honest in their dealings, no matter how strong the temptations may be to try to profit through bribes or other illicit means. Imagine a world where all political and business leaders conducted themselves as God directs!

In Proverbs 1:10-19, we have Solomon's well-known admonition to his son to avoid being drawn by evil associates into a life of theft and violence. Even those who are "innocent" of wrongdoing can be implicated as accessories in the crimes of their associates. Greed is pictured here as the motivation for these sins, but sometimes otherwise good people are drawn into such things by peer pressure, or a desire to be accepted by others. Although it may be unusual for Christians to fall into a life of violent crime, crimes like shoplifting are much too common. No matter how exciting and "profitable" crime may seem, verses 18 and 19 provide a clear picture of the conclusion of such a story – the greedy criminals hurt not only their victims, but themselves, as well. Notice particularly verse 19: "So are the ways of *everyone* who is greedy for gain; it takes away the life of its owners." [Emphasis added]. As the Lord tells us, we cannot serve God and wealth. If our lives are driven by greed, we are no longer in control – we have become slaves to material things. This is a prescription for losing our spiritual lives, as well. We should also remember that greed is an "equal opportunity vice" in that it can afflict both the rich and poor alike.

Greedy people tend to have greedy people around them. When a person's drive for wealth is temporarily successful, there will be plenty of "friends" there to help spend the money. However, just as in the story of the prodigal son, when the money goes, the greedy friends go with it, leaving only loneliness and despair. Wealth, like power, fame, and good looks, is a very flimsy basis for a relationship.

In Proverbs 19:10, Solomon describes two incongruities: a fool with luxuries, and a servant in power over princes. People who make wealth their goal often have no idea how to deal with wealth. "A fool and his money are soon parted" is a truism. It is sad to watch a shallow, greedy person obtain some wealth and have no idea how to use it properly. God has a plan for how His people should use wealth, but greedy people, of course, are not interested in the plans of God. We need to learn and apply God's lessons for using wealth so that we don't behave like fools with the money God gives us.

We close this section with a look at Proverbs 25:16. It would be easy for us to read right over this verse and miss its powerful, and much needed, modern applications. Envision the society of Israel in Solomon's day. The vast majority of the people work hard to provide a meager subsistence living for themselves and their families. Every meal involves hard work. In this environment, finding honey would be quite an event – a delicious, nutritious meal available with no work required! Furthermore, unlike milk, meat, and many other foodstuffs in the days before refrigeration, honey could be preserved for a long period. This is a windfall – comparable in our day to an unexpected inheritance, contest winnings, or other pleasant financial surprise.

How does Solomon say we should react to such a windfall? The fool in Solomon's day would gorge himself until sick, leaving nothing for later. Many people in our day behave just as foolishly. The applicable cliché is "easy come, easy go." How much wiser it would be to enjoy some modest portion of the windfall, while putting much of it back for later use! Once again, we should marvel at the wisdom before us, and the relevance it has to our world three thousand years after it was spoken.

Be Careful Not to Oppress the Poor

If the rich forget what is most important and become overcome with pride and driven by greed, they are likely to try to take advantage of those who are less fortunate. This has happened throughout history, and was certainly common in Old Testament times. The prophets repeatedly denounced the rich and powerful in Israel for abusing the poor. (See, for example, Isaiah 3:13-15; Amos 2:6-7; Micah 3:2-3). Solomon was familiar with this tendency, and knew how much God despised such behavior. He issues numerous warnings to God's people about the practice.

He who oppresses the poor to increase his riches, and he who gives to the rich, will surely come to poverty.
Proverbs 22:16

52   Solomon on Wealth

> Do not rob the poor because he is poor, nor oppress the afflicted at the gate; for the Lord will plead their cause, and plunder the soul of those who plunder them.
>
> Proverbs 22:22-23

> He will judge Your people with righteousness, and Your poor with justice. The mountains will bring peace to the people, and the little hills, by righteousness. He will bring justice to the poor of the people; He will save the children of the needy, and will break in pieces the oppressor.
>
> Psalm 72:2-4

> For He will deliver the needy when he cries, the poor also, and him who has no helper. He will spare the poor and needy, and will save the souls of the needy. He will redeem their life from oppression and violence; and precious shall be their blood in His sight.
>
> Psalm 72:12-14

> One who increases his possessions by usury and extortion gathers it for him who will pity the poor.
>
> Proverbs 28:8

> Like a roaring lion and a charging bear is a wicked ruler over poor people. A ruler who lacks understanding is a great oppressor, but he who hates covetousness will prolong his days.
>
> Proverbs 28:15-16

Solomon tells us that taking advantage of people does not pay in the long run. People who try to gain wealth this way "will surely come to poverty." Those who give to the rich are also promised poverty. Someone might suppose that they can gain some advantage by ingratiating themselves to the rich, but these rich are the greedy rich. They will not feel the need to help those who give to them – they will simply take those gifts and use them for themselves.

We are told that the Lord will plead the cause of the poor and afflicted, and will plunder the soul of those who plunder them. Those who oppress the poor are literally trying to fight against God. They will not prevail!

Solomon condemns the practice of usury, or high rates of interest, particularly when charged to the poor. Israelites were forbidden from charging usury to their brethren, and were always entreated to be generous to the poor. How do you think God views those of our day who would attempt to get rich by preying on the poor? What does this say about Christians running financial institutions that charge exorbitant rates of interest, and whose clientele are primarily the poor? Can we really think God is pleased with this? Solomon says no!

Those who are in positions of power over the poor – particularly politicians and business owners and/or managers – have a special responsibility to treat the poor with care and concern. God is truly pleased with rich and powerful Christians who behave toward the poor as He directs.

Points to Remember

Solomon says a lot about understanding the proper priorities of life. Wealth presents a real danger in pulling our attention away from spiritual things toward material things. The pursuit of wealth can lead to a person falling prey to get-rich-quick schemes, which, Solomon says, never work. Workaholism is another danger for those who are too enamored with possessions. Solomon warns that such a life is not fulfilling, and not what God wants for His people. Another danger that often comes with wealth is pride. Pride is always spoken against in God's Word. The rich person who becomes proud of his possessions or station in life will probably not trust God as he should. Solomon wants us to remember that riches will fly away!

Wealthy people often become greedy. The accumulation of wealth may lead to a burning desire for more. This can lead to all sorts of misery, and is likely to result in the greedy person mistreating others in order to gain more wealth. God's people are to show love and concern for the needy, and must never abuse the poor in any way.

We even saw Solomon discuss the right way to handle an economic windfall (Proverbs 25:16). Unexpected good fortune is a blessing from God, and should be used as God directs. Just as with all our blessings, we should be careful not to waste or "blow" such blessings. Rather, they represent a special opportunity to provide for our needs, as well as the needs of others. As always, Solomon encourages us to use wisdom in such circumstances.

Chapter 5

Work diligently

He who has a slack hand becomes poor, but the hand of the diligent makes rich. He who gathers in summer is a wise son; he who sleeps in harvest is a son who causes shame.

Proverbs 10:4-5

God's plans are always the best plans. God wants His people to understand that material blessings come from Him, and that they should be used in His service. If we use our wealth in the way God prescribes, we can avoid the potential dangers that were discussed in the preceding chapter.

In the three preceding chapters, we looked at passages where Solomon teaches us about wealth – that it is a blessing from God, that it is not the most important of God's blessings, and that it can be a danger. In the next four chapters, we will see some specific actions that Solomon teaches us to take that relate to wealth.

In this chapter, we will focus on God's plan for how we obtain wealth. The plan is very simple. God wants His people to work diligently. As Steven Scott points out in his book, *The Richest Man Who Ever Lived*, diligence is more than just hard work; it is a combination of hard work and wisdom.[1] God promises us that diligence will be rewarded. On the other hand, He warns us against the folly of laziness. Interestingly, Solomon had more to say on the need for diligence, and the foolishness of laziness, than on any other subject in our study. Solomon knew what a strong temptation laziness can be, and how much some people would want to avoid work. The question for us is, will we follow God's clear plan, or will we look for some "easy" path to wealth?

Diligence Will Be Rewarded

Life is short. In the short time we are given, God asks us to work with diligence on the things that are important. He also promises us that He will reward our efforts when we work diligently, as long as our motives are proper.

Do you see a man who excels in his work? He will stand before kings; he will not stand before unknown men.
Proverbs 22:29

Work Diligently 57

Where no oxen are, the trough is clean; but much increase comes by the strength of an ox.

Proverbs 14:4

The person who labors, labors for himself, for his hungry mouth drives him on.

Proverbs 16:26

Prepare your outside work, make it fit for yourself in the field; and afterward build your house.

Proverbs 24:27

Be diligent to know the state of your flocks, and attend to your herds; for riches are not forever, nor does a crown endure to all generations. When the hay is removed, and the tender grass shows itself, and the herbs of the mountains are gathered in, the lambs will provide your clothing, and the goats the price of a field; you shall have enough goats' milk for your food, for the food of your household, and the nourishment of your maidservants.

Proverbs 27:23-27

Whatever your hand finds to do, do it with your might; for there is no work or device or knowledge or wisdom in the grave where you are going.

Ecclesiastes 9:10

In the morning sow your seed, and in the evening do not withhold your hand; for you do not know which will prosper, either this or that, or whether both alike will be good.

Ecclesiastes 11:6

When people work diligently, they will generally prosper. Solomon says that those who excel in their work will stand before kings. This reminds the Bible student of men like Joseph, whose faithful service in Egypt resulted in his being made second only to the pharaoh, and Daniel, who served the kings of Babylon and Persia.

Practically speaking, there are times when hardworking servants of God do not "get ahead" in some work environments. There are numerous reasons why this may happen. Righteous people may shy away from the self-promotion that helps some people climb the organizational ladder. Certainly, we should not participate in the dishonest practices that some people use to advance themselves. It is often frustrating for God's people to see the unrighteous succeeding, perhaps even at our expense. However, we should take heart when we realize that our spiritual lives are more important than our work lives, and that, ultimately, God's plan for success always works.

Proverbs 14:4 speaks eloquently of the importance of priorities in our work. Solomon paints us a picture of a farmer who has a clean barn that could serve as a showplace. The problem, of course, is that the barn is so clean because there are no animals that use it. What good is a spotless barn that is never used by animals? On the other hand, a barn where oxen are kept will not be spotless, but the work of the oxen provides increase for their owner.

There are lessons here for us. Some people spend all their time and energies on things that keep them busy, but that really do not matter much. They may have homes that are showplaces, lawns that look like they belong in a magazine, and bodies that are always perfectly toned, but they may never "have time" for hospitality, or for instructing their children in God's ways, or helping the needy, or working to bring someone to Christ. What good is that perfect house or lawn, really? Furthermore, all these efforts directed toward having a "clean trough" can lead to increased stress, which may result in poor job performance. We certainly need to be hard at work, but we must be working with the right set of priorities in mind.

Proverbs 24:27 also speaks to our priorities in a very practical way. Solomon says that a man should prepare his outside work, such as his fields, first, before building his house. A man's fields provided his income. If he did not prepare his fields and get his seed planted, he would have no revenue. Imagine what the people of Solomon's day would think of a man who failed to plant his crop at the proper time because he was busy building a nice home. How much pleasure would the nice house be as he starved during the winter? You can live in a tent or a lean-to, but you must eat!

In our day, we often see people who want a beautiful home and comfortable – perhaps extravagant – lifestyle before they have the income to support it. Young people, particularly, often want a lifestyle equal to, or better than, that of their parents, even though their parents may have spent many years reaching that point. Furthermore, debt is the typical method these young people would use for achieving this lifestyle. We will see more in the next chapter about what Solomon says about the problems that debt brings. We need to remember that God does not promise us instant success and wealth. In fact, that is most definitely *not* his plan! The time for us to reap rewards is after our income is secured by our labors.

One of the clearest Biblical admonitions for diligence in financial management is found in Proverbs 27:23-27. Solomon encourages his readers to be diligent to know the state of their flocks and attend to their herds. God's people should spend time in making sure that their financial assets are used effectively. If our assets are taken care of, Solomon tells us, they will then take care of us and provide for our future.

Some Christians have misinterpreted passages such as Matthew 6:25-34, and teach that we must take no thought for our financial futures. Perhaps this misunderstanding results from the reading of the King James Version, which says "take therefore no thought for the morrow" (Matthew 6:34). The newer translations render the thought more accurately as "therefore do not worry about tomorrow" (New King James Version) or "be not therefore anxious for the morrow" (American Standard Version). This passage is not a warning against financial planning, but against worry or anxiety over the future. Of course, we are to put our trust in God in all things, but God clearly expects us to think about, plan for, and take action regarding, financial concerns, as Solomon makes plain to us here. Budgeting, retirement planning, investing, buying insurance, and other types of financial planning do *not* necessarily reflect a lack of trust in God, but rather should be a part of a Christian's diligence in acting as an effective steward of the financial blessings that come from God and as a provider for his or her family.

God's people are to be hard workers. Ecclesiastes 9:10 reminds us that now is the time given to us to accomplish things. We have no guarantee of another day, and no work can be done after death. Jesus certainly possessed this sense of urgency in His spiritual work. In John 9:4, He said, "I must work the works of Him who sent Me while it is day; the night is coming when no one can work." The Christian should feel this same sense of urgency about his spiritual work first, but also about his physical work. Laziness, as we shall see, gets us nowhere.

In Ecclesiastes 11:6, Solomon seems to be talking not just about hard work (in the morning and evening), but perhaps also about diversification of our labor. In the morning, the Israelite could work outside, doing tasks such as sowing his seed. In the evening, he is encouraged to keep working. Apparently, this would be some sort of inside work, after sundown. The wise man argues for this diversification by saying that "you do not know which will prosper." There are several good applications for us. We might encourage our children, for example, to obtain and cultivate multiple skills. We see this in the apostle Paul who generally worked as an evangelist, but could also support himself through his skill as a tentmaker.

Solomon's instructions here would also argue for diversification in investments, as opposed to approaches that could be described as "putting all our eggs in one basket." Just like the Israelite farmer, we never know which of our efforts will prosper. In spite of Solomon's warnings, we still see Christians who pour all their financial assets into a single investment – certain that the stock price will increase or the real estate market will continue to rise. Virtually all reputable financial managers will strongly encourage diversification of effort and investment. It appears that Solomon is telling us that they are right.

Laziness is Foolish

As we have seen, Solomon speaks often of the wisdom of working hard, and of the rewards that come from diligence. He also makes the negative argument by pointing out the "rewards" of laziness.

> Go to the ant, you sluggard! Consider her ways and be wise, which, having no captain, overseer or ruler, provides her supplies in the summer, and gathers her food in the harvest. How long will you slumber, O sluggard? When will you rise from your sleep? A little sleep, a little slumber, a little folding of the hands to sleep – so shall your poverty come on you like a prowler, and your need like an armed man.
>
> **Proverbs 6:6-11**

> I went by the field of the lazy man, and by the vineyard of the man devoid of understanding; and there it was, all overgrown with thorns; its surface was covered with nettles; its stone wall was broken down. When I saw it, I considered it well; I looked on it and received instruction: a little sleep, a little slumber, a little folding of the hands to rest; so shall your poverty come like a prowler, and your need like an armed man.
>
> **Proverbs 24:30-34**

> Much food is in the fallow ground of the poor, and for lack of justice there is waste.
>
> **Proverbs 13:23**

> The lazy man will not plow because of winter; he will beg during harvest and have nothing.
>
> Proverbs 20:4
>
> He who is slothful in his work is a brother to him who is a great destroyer.
>
> Proverbs 18:9
>
> Because of laziness the building decays, and through idleness of hands the house leaks.
>
> Ecclesiastes 10:18

Solomon asks the man who would be lazy to consider the example of the ant. The ants need no overseer to drive them, but are self-motivated. In Colossians 3:22-24, Paul encourages servants to work hard, "not with eyeservice, as men-pleasers ... [but] heartily, as to the Lord and not to men." Christians should not need to be driven and cajoled to work. We should not be the type of employees who slack off when the boss is not around, and who work hard only to impress others. We work for the Lord! All our talents, all our abilities, all our time – everything we can give – is to be freely given in His service. The ants also work continually, knowing that winter is on its way. Again, we see the admonition to prepare for the future while we can. It doesn't take much laziness to result in poverty and financial distress!

The neglected field is a powerful picture of the results of laziness. The field, if managed well and worked diligently, could be the provider of wealth for its owner. The overgrown field, with broken-down walls, as observed by Solomon, serves only as a monument to the owner's laziness and a warning to others of the danger of slothfulness. Those whose lives are characterized by laziness and frivolity earn for themselves and their families a legacy of poverty and financial difficulties. God must be particularly disgusted by those people who are too lazy to work to better their circumstances, as He directs, but are quick to blame others – family, friends, the government, God Himself – for their condition!

Diligence and Laziness Contrasted

Solomon wants to make sure we get his message – diligence is what God expects of us. In the rest of this chapter, we will see diligence contrasted with laziness, with frivolity, and with dishonesty.

> He who has a slack hand becomes poor, but the hand of the diligent makes rich. He who gathers in summer is a wise son; he who sleeps in harvest is a son who causes shame.
> **Proverbs 10:4-5**

> The hand of the diligent will rule, but the lazy man will be put to forced labor.
> **Proverbs 12:24**

> The soul of a lazy man desires and has nothing; but the soul of the diligent shall be made rich.
> **Proverbs 13:4**

The lazy man does not roast what he took in hunting, but diligence is man's precious possession.
Proverbs 12:27

Do not love sleep, lest you come to poverty; open your eyes, and you will be satisfied with bread.
Proverbs 20:13

The desire of the lazy man kills him, for his hands refuse to labor. He covets greedily all day long, but the righteous gives and does not spare.
Proverbs 21:25-26

From these passages, we see several rewards for the diligent – wealth, the approval of their loved ones, promotion, provision of necessities, and an abundance that can be shared. On the other hand, the lazy man earns poverty, shame, forced labor, unfulfilled desires, and a life of frustration. The choice is so clear, yet so many people – including some Christians – feel that they have a better plan than God's plan.

Note Proverbs 12:27, in particular. Have you ever started a worthy task and failed to follow through with it? All of us have. Solomon speaks of the lazy man who kills an animal and then fails to cook the meat, which would then spoil. When we buy a product that has a rebate and fail to mail the rebate in, we are being just as lazy as this hunter. When we get some information about a sale on a needed item or a favorable investment opportunity, and then fail to act on it in time, we are letting the meat spoil.

Diligence and Frivolity Contrasted

Hard work is not necessarily our favorite course of action. Having fun is, well, more fun! Children, when left to themselves, will almost always choose play over work. We ought to teach our children to work hard, but some of us adults have never "grown up" in this regard! Does it infuriate you to see grown men and women who behave like children when it comes to work and play? They want to own every toy ever invented, and they usually have to borrow money to get them, since they spend all their time playing with their toys, rather than working. They want to spend every available minute in front of the television or computer game, or on the river or the golf course, rather than using their time productively in work or self-improvement. If we find such behavior in others to be disappointing – as we should – how do we think God feels about it? Listen to Solomon as he tells us how God feels about it.

He who tills his land will be satisfied with bread, but he who follows frivolity is devoid of understanding.
Proverbs 12:11

He who tills his land will have plenty of bread, but he who follows frivolity will have poverty enough!
Proverbs 28:19

In all labor there is profit, but idle chatter leads only to poverty.
Proverbs 14:23

He who loves pleasure will be a poor man; he who loves wine and oil will not be rich.
Proverbs 21:17

Do not mix with winebibbers, or with gluttonous eaters of meat; for the drunkard and the glutton will come to poverty, and drowsiness will clothe a man with rags.
Proverbs 23:20-21

The rewards of diligence are satisfaction, plenty, and profit. Frivolity yields short-lived pleasure, but ultimately brings poverty. When we follow God's plan and work diligently, we will please God, and we will be the right kind of examples to our children, our fellow Christians, and those outside of Christ.

Diligence and Dishonesty Contrasted

God's people are to increase wealth through diligent effort – never through dishonesty. The cliché "honesty is the best policy" is a very Biblical idea. Dishonesty was rampant in ancient Israel, just as it is today. Solomon's warnings are still needed in a world filled with all sorts of dishonest business practices, including insider trading, embezzlement, securities fraud, and income tax evasion.

Wealth gained by dishonesty will be diminished, but he who gathers by labor will increase.

Proverbs 13:11

The plans of the diligent lead surely to plenty, but those of everyone who is hasty, surely to poverty. Getting treasures by a lying tongue is the fleeting fantasy of those who seek death.

Proverbs 21:5-6

Honest weights and scales are the Lord's; all the weights in the bag are His work.

Proverbs 16:11

Do not remove the ancient landmark which your fathers have set.

Proverbs 22:28

Do not remove the ancient landmark, nor enter the fields of the fatherless; for their Redeemer is mighty; He will plead their cause against you.

Proverbs 23:10-11

Even when dishonesty does lead to wealth, that wealth tends to disappear when the dishonesty is discovered, as it usually is. Consider the financial circumstances faced by the wife and children of a man sentenced to a long prison term because of white-collar crime. The major breadwinner's income is gone, large financial restitution and penalties must be paid, and the financial outlook upon his release is bleak, as well. Of course, these financial consequences fall on top of the emotional and spiritual fallout from the sin. Truly, people who choose a dishonest path to wealth often discover that it is "the fleeting fantasy of those who seek death."

Larry Burkett, in *Business by the Book*, tells of merchants in ancient Israel who carried two sets of weights to use when measuring grain for their customers – one honest set for rich customers, who were likely to have their own weights to compare, and one dishonest set for poor customers, who had no way to compare.[2] Such practices were, and are, despicable to God not only because they are dishonest, but also because they are designed to abuse the poor. In Proverbs 16:11, Solomon says that all the weights in the bag are the Lord's work. The center-column note in the New King James Bible says they are the Lord's "concern." God expects His people to be honest in all dealings with others, but special care should be taken to treat the poor fairly and honestly, as well as with kindness and compassion.

The last two passages above instruct us not to "remove the ancient landmark." The landmark would represent an agreement between neighbors about the location of the property line. Agreements and contracts are serious matters, and Christians must view them as such. Especially grievous conduct in this regard would be attempting to take advantage of vulnerable people, such as orphans. God is always concerned with the plight of the unfortunate, and He expects His people to have this concern also. The poor may feel like they have no one looking out for them, but Solomon tells us that God will plead their cause. Those who sell unneeded insurance to the elderly, who charge outrageous rates of interest to the poor, or take advantage of the unfortunate in any way, will not escape God's judgment!

Points to Remember

Solomon wants us to understand that, for the people of God, the key to building wealth should be hard work. Furthermore, he tells us that diligent effort and careful financial management is a plan that will work. As Dave Ramsey says, "work is a surefire moneymaking scheme!"[3] Diligent effort will be rewarded, but we must remember to manage and use our money wisely, and with the proper priorities. With respect to financial priorities, Solomon points out the need to make sure we have an income established before spending effort and money on a nice new house or other distractions.

We need to remember the principle of diversification in financial effort. Some things are beyond our control, but God asks us to be diligent about those things we can control. Having a skill to fall back on in the event of a job loss, having life, disability, and health insurance, having savings in different types of investments – all these represent wise actions in preparing for life's unexpected events. Taking reasonable precautions to guard against financial risk does *not* show a lack of trust in God, but rather demonstrates good stewardship of the blessings God has given us.

Laziness and devotion to frivolity are signs of immaturity. Godly parents understand the importance of helping their children learn to grow out of these childish behaviors. Unfortunately, many people never learn this! According to Solomon, laziness and frivolity lead ultimately, and perhaps quickly, to financial ruin. In contrast, diligent effort leads to financial blessings. Voltaire said that "work keeps us from three evils: boredom, vice, and poverty."[4] Dishonesty has no place in the life of the Christian. Attempting to achieve financial gain through dishonesty and taking advantage of others is not only a violation of God's law; it is also not a good plan for building wealth, even from a human perspective. Wealth gained through dishonesty, Solomon tells us, will be diminished.

Chapter 6

Avoid debt

The rich rules over the poor, and the borrower is servant to the lender.

Proverbs 22:7

As we saw from the statistics presented in chapter one, debt is a significant and growing problem in our society. Most church leaders would agree that many Christians with whom they work face these same sorts of financial problems. Debt is often one of the most serious symptoms of the financial difficulties that people experience.

Note that I refer to debt as a symptom. Debt is a result of financial problems such as (1) greed, (2) failure to plan for the future, (3) careless financial management, or (4) an unforeseeable catastrophic financial event. The first three of these problems, in turn, generally result from a more fundamental cause – immaturity. As we have seen, Solomon's counsel is designed to produce wisdom, which will lead us to spiritual – and financial - maturity.

Solomon had less to say directly about debt than about the issues we discuss in the other chapters of this book, so we will be looking at fewer passages from Proverbs and Ecclesiastes in this chapter than we have in the other chapters. However, what Solomon says about debt is highly significant and enlightening.

After looking at what Solomon says about debt, we will also look at passages on debt from other parts of Scripture. This is a departure from what we have been doing in other chapters, but I believe it is needed here, for several reasons. First, as mentioned above, debt is such a huge problem for so many people today, including the people of God. Second, as we will see, the Scriptures teach very plainly and consistently on this topic, and looking at what Solomon says along with the other passages will make these lessons abundantly clear. Finally, there seems to be a significant amount of misinformation and confusion in the religious world, and we need to make sure we grasp God's attitude toward debt, so that we can approach this subject in a godly way.

The Borrower is Slave to the Lender

In this section, we will focus on a single short passage, but it is, I believe, one of the most significant passages in our study.

> The rich rules over the poor, and the borrower is servant to the lender.
>
> Proverbs 22:7

You will note that the New King James Version has the word "servant," yet I have used the word "slave" in the section heading. I have done this intentionally. Some translations (e.g., the New American Standard Bible) have "slave," rather than "servant." A search in an exhaustive concordance will show "slave" and "bondservant" as synonyms for this word. The idea of bondage is included in this word in the original language.

Americans profess to love freedom. None of us wants to think of ourselves as a slave. The word "servant" sounds so much nicer – so much nobler! The thought that God is trying to get across to us, though, is that a person who borrows places himself in bondage to the lender. Yet so many of us rush to the lenders, begging to become their slaves!

This is a passage that some people may go to great lengths to try to "get around." They may talk about how debtors in Bible times were sometimes sold into slavery (e.g., see Matthew 18:30), and suggest that this is the bondage referred to here. I do not believe that is what this proverb is referring to, and neither do the commentators I have read. I believe Solomon is presenting a truism here – a statement that describes the relationship between borrowers and lenders in general. When we attempt to "get around" this most obvious meaning of the passage, it may indicate an emotional response on our part. If we do not like what the passage is saying, we may be severely tempted to refuse to acknowledge the plain and simple truth of it!

Why is Solomon's statement a truism? If I owe money to a bank, a finance company, or an individual, I am obligated scripturally to repay that debt (Psalm 37:21). Obviously, that means that some portion of my labor each day is given to that lender, rather than to God, my family, others, or myself. Some might object and point out that the loan simply provided funds for the purchase of an item that I may need. Even if that point were conceded, the interest charges on the loan are simply profit to the lender, and are only needed to finance the debt. In other words, if I save and pay cash for the item, there are no interest charges owed.

Debt robs us of financial freedom. How many young (or not so young) couples sit down to review a budget and realize that their debt obligations have removed most, or all, of the "slack" in their budgets? They do not have the freedom to save as much as they would like for the future, to give as they would like to God or the needy, or to simply cover unexpected events. Their debt is like a strait jacket, which will not allow them to use their financial resources as God would want.

God wants His people to be free. Freedom from sin should be our foremost concern, of course, but I believe the Scriptures plainly teach that God also wants us to be free from the stress, worry, and limitations that debt brings to our lives. As we continue this chapter, I hope that will become even clearer.

Avoid Surety at All Costs

Solomon discusses, at surprising length, what he calls "surety." Some writers have said that he is referring to debt, in general, but I do not think the text really supports that interpretation. Author Ron Blue, in his book *Master Your Money*, says that "[s]urety in itself is not debt, but it is rather guaranteeing the debt of another."[1] The most common type of surety in our time is co-signing a loan. Let us look at what Solomon has to say about this.

> Do not be one of those who shakes hands in a pledge, one of those who is surety for debts; if you have nothing with which to pay, why should he take away your bed from under you?
> **Proverbs 22:26-27**
>
> He who is surety for a stranger will suffer, but one who hates being surety is secure.
> **Proverbs 11:15**
>
> Take the garment of one who is surety for a stranger, and hold it as a pledge when it is for a seductress.
> **Proverbs 20:16**
>
> Take the garment of him who is surety for a stranger, and hold it in pledge when he is surety for a seductress.
> **Proverbs 27:13**

Solomon on Wealth

> A man devoid of understanding shakes hands in a pledge, and becomes surety for his friend.
>
> Proverbs 17:18
>
> My son, if you become surety for your friend, if you have shaken hands in pledge for a stranger, you are snared by the words of your mouth. So do this, my son, and deliver yourself; for you have come into the hand of your friend: go and humble yourself; plead with your friend. Give no sleep to your eyes, nor slumber to your eyelids. Deliver yourself like a gazelle from the hand of the hunter, and like a bird from the hand of the fowler.
>
> Proverbs 6:1-5

According to Solomon, co-signing a loan is foolishness. Solomon says that you should not be surety for debts – neither for a stranger, nor even for a friend. Financial institutions in our time are eager to loan money. Credit card companies offer their debt to teens, to bankrupt individuals, and sometimes even to dead people and pets! If they require someone to have a co-signer, it usually means that they have strong evidence that the person will not be able to repay the loan. If you agree to co-sign for them, you should expect to be called upon to repay the loan yourself! Why, Solomon asks, should you lose your property because of someone else's debt?

Notice Solomon's instructions, in Proverbs 6:1-5, to those who have agreed to act as surety. They should do everything they can to be released from this obligation. They should deliver themselves from it "like a gazelle from the hand of the hunter, and like a bird from the hand of the fowler." A wise person will simply avoid serving as a guaranty for someone else's debt.

Consider another important implication of the instructions regarding surety. God's people are to serve others. What if a brother or sister in Christ cannot get a loan? Shouldn't I serve them by agreeing to co-sign for them? Solomon says "no!" How can a godly person turn his or her back on this needy one? He shouldn't, of course! If someone needs our help, we need to be willing to sacrifice to help him or her. My conclusion is that co-signing a loan for them is not the kind of help God wants us to give them. In fact, it is not really "help," at all! If they really, desperately, need this money, and we are able to help them, we should give them money, rather than trying to help them by increasing their debt. We will learn more about our responsibility to help others in the next chapter.

Finally, if debt is not good for this needy brother or sister, as I have argued above, why is it good for me? I believe Solomon wants us to realize the dangers associated with debt, and learn to avoid them. In the next section, we will look at other Scriptures that support this contention.

What the Bible Says About Debt

As mentioned above, we will now examine some debt-related verses from other parts of the Bible. There are many other passages on debt, but those discussed below provide a fairly comprehensive picture of how God wants us to view debt. Readers desiring to study this subject in more detail may want to read Larry

Burkett's *Debt-Free Living*, which includes an appendix that lists and classifies all the credit-related passages in the Scriptures.

> The wicked borrows and does not repay, but the righteous shows mercy and gives.
>
> Psalm 37:21

> I have been young, and now am old; yet I have not seen the righteous forsaken, nor his descendants begging bread. He is ever merciful, and lends; and his descendants are blessed.
>
> Psalm 37:25-26

> Now it shall come to pass, if you diligently obey the voice of the Lord your God, to observe carefully all His commandments which I command you today, that the Lord your God will set you high above all nations of the earth.... The Lord will open to you His good treasure, the heavens, to give the rain to your land in its season, and to bless all the work of your hand. You shall lend to many nations, but you shall not borrow.
>
> Deuteronomy 28:1,12

> But it shall come to pass, if you do not obey the voice of the Lord your God, to observe carefully all His commandments and His statutes which I command you today, that all these curses will come upon you and overtake you: ... The alien who is among you shall rise higher and higher above you, and you shall come down lower and lower. He shall lend to you, but you shall not lend to him; he shall be the head, and you shall be the tail.
>
> Deuteronomy 28:15, 43-44

For the Lord your God will bless you just as He promised you; you shall lend to many nations, but you shall not borrow; you shall reign over many nations, but they shall not reign over you.
Deuteronomy 15:6

You shall not charge interest to your brother – interest on money or food or anything that is lent out at interest. To a foreigner you may charge interest, but to your brother you shall not charge interest, that the Lord your God may bless you in all to which you set your hand in the land which you are entering to possess.
Deuteronomy 23:19-20

A certain woman of the wives of the sons of the prophets cried out to Elisha, saying, "Your servant my husband is dead, and you know that your servant feared the Lord. And the creditor is coming to take my two sons to be his slaves." So Elisha said to her, "What shall I do for you? Tell me, what do you have in the house?" And she said, "Your maidservant has nothing in the house but a jar of oil." Then he said, "Go, borrow vessels from everywhere, from all your neighbors – empty vessels; do not gather just a few. And when you have come in, you shall shut the door behind you and your sons; then pour it into all those vessels, and set aside the full ones." So she went from him and shut the door behind her and her sons, who brought the vessels to her; and she poured it out. Now it came to pass, when the vessels were full, that she said to her son, "Bring me another vessel." And he said to her, "There is not another vessel." So the oil ceased. Then she came and told the man of God. And he said, "Go, sell the oil and pay your debt; and you and your sons live on the rest."
II Kings 4:1-7

> Render therefore to all their due: taxes to whom taxes are due, customs to whom customs, fear to whom fear, honor to whom honor. Owe no one anything except to love one another, for he who loves another has fulfilled the law.
>
> Romans 13:7-8

The passages above teach us the following lessons about debt:

- Christians must always repay their debts.
- Loaning money is not wrong, and can be a demonstration of mercy. Therefore, borrowing money must not be wrong.
- One of the curses God placed upon His disobedient people was putting them in a position where they were forced to borrow money from surrounding nations. Conversely, if God's people followed His will, He promised to enable them to be lenders to other nations, rather than borrowers. This illustrates that being in debt is an undesirable state of affairs!
- God did not want His people to charge interest on loans to their brothers.
- In desperate circumstances, the widow had become indebted. When she had money from the sale of the miraculously-produced oil, the prophet told her to go first and repay her debts. This would indicate that becoming debt free must be a high financial priority.

Some believe that Romans 13:8 is a prohibition on all debt. I do not believe that this is the case. Rather, the context would indicate that this is an instruction to pay any and all obligations (e.g., taxes, customs, honor), and to show love in all our dealings with others.

Points to Remember

Debt usually results from one of the following: (1) greed, (2) failure to plan for the future, (3) careless financial management, or (4) an unforeseeable catastrophic financial event. If you have debt, it may be illuminating to think about what has caused it.

The Bible does not teach that debt is a sin, but it *never* presents debt in a favorable light. Specifically, the Scriptures teach (1) that the borrower is slave to the lender, (2) that debt is generally foolish, (3) that we should not serve as surety for someone else's debt, (4) that debt causes a loss of financial freedom, (5) that God used indebtedness to curse Israel when they were disobedient, and (6) that debt should be repaid as soon as possible. Additionally, the story of the widow's oil seems to indicate that debt is a desperate, "last-resort" response to a financial catastrophe (in the widow's case, the loss of her husband).

Since Solomon and the other inspired writers consistently present debt as undesirable, Christians should be very reluctant to incur debt, and should make every effort to pay any debt off as soon as possible. To use debt routinely to feed the impulses of greed, or because of careless financial planning or management, is foolishness, according to Solomon. Which pattern do we want to follow – the "American way," or God's way?

Chapter 7

Help others

He who has pity on the poor lends to the Lord, and He will pay back what he has given.

Proverbs 19:17

God expects His people to help others. As Dave Ramsey says, God is a giver, and we are made in His image. If we are to be like God, we must be givers also.[1] Solomon has much to say about the need for us to be generous, giving people, in order to please God.

Take Opportunities to Help Others

In the last two chapters, we saw that Solomon tells us that we need to work diligently and avoid debt. If we fail to be diligent and manage our financial resources well, or if we are saddled with large debt, we will have difficulty in helping meet the needs of other people when opportunities arise – and such opportunities are almost always available, if we are watching for them. Being generous – at least on a consistent basis – requires planning. It is difficult to respond to the needs of others when our own finances are a mess.

On the other hand, it can be a real joy to plan to help others, and to be ready when an opportunity presents itself. Financial counselor Ron Blue reports that his clients' giving goes up, on average, by a factor of four when they develop plans to give, compared with what they were giving before doing such planning.[2]

> Do not withhold good from those to whom it is due, when it is in the power of your hand to do so. Do not say to your neighbor, "Go and come back, and tomorrow I will give it," when you have it with you.
> **Proverbs 3:27-28**

I believe the passage above means that we need to be prepared to respond quickly to someone who is in need. How ready are you to respond to the needs of others, especially those opportunities that may arise on the spur of the moment? We will talk more in chapter ten about a practical way to implement this instruction.

This passage also has application to the repayment of debts. Failure to repay a debt in a timely fashion could certainly be considered "withhold[ing] good from those to whom it is due." Too often, people make conscious decisions to delay repayment of a debt beyond the time that has been agreed to. There is simply no excuse for those who would abuse the patience and trust of others in this way.

Generosity Leads to Blessings

Expecting to be blessed is a selfish motive for giving. God's people should be giving people primarily because of their love for God and for others. However, Solomon does teach that God will bless His children if they are generous to others.

He who has pity on the poor lends to the Lord, and He will pay back what he has given.
Proverbs 19:17

He who has a generous eye will be blessed, for he gives of his bread to the poor.
Proverbs 22:9

If your enemy is hungry, give him bread to eat; and if he is thirsty, give him water to drink; for so you will heap coals of fire on his head, and the Lord will reward you.
Proverbs 25:21-22

Cast your bread upon the waters, for you will find it after many days. Give a serving to seven, and also to eight, for you do not know what evil will be on the earth.
Ecclesiastes 11:1-2

It would be hard to overstate the significance of Proverbs 19:17. Solomon says that when we help the poor we are lending to the Lord. Can you imagine a better kind of investment than lending to the Lord? Remember what Jesus said in His description of the judgment scene in Matthew 25:40 regarding service to those in need, "Assuredly, I say to you, inasmuch as you did it to one of the least of these My brethren, you did it to Me."

We must not think, of course, that we can earn salvation by our good works, such as by showing generosity to the poor. God expects His people to have an obedient faith in Him (see, for example, James 2:14-26), but even when we have done everything God commands, we are still unprofitable servants (Luke 17:10), wholly dependant on the grace of God.

Solomon even says that we are to be generous to our enemies. Paul quotes this proverb in Romans 12:20, then encourages us to "overcome evil with good." God will reward this kind of selflessness, and the enemy may be moved by shame to repent of the ill will he feels toward the righteous one.

Generosity and Greed Contrasted

Greed is selfishness. Generosity is selflessness. God has given abundantly to us, and He asks us to emulate His generosity in the way we deal with others. If we desire to be more like God, we will desire to give to help others.

There is one who scatters, yet increases more; and there is one who withholds more than is right, but it leads to poverty. The generous soul will be made rich, and he who waters will also be watered himself. The people will curse him who withholds grain, but blessing will be on the head of him who sells it.

Proverbs 11:24-26

The desire of the lazy man kills him, for his hands refuse to labor. He covets greedily all day long, but the righteous gives and does not spare.

Proverbs 21:25-26

He who gives to the poor will not lack, but he who hides his eyes will have many curses.

Proverbs 28:27

The righteous considers the cause of the poor, but the wicked does not understand such knowledge.

Proverbs 29:7

The irony of the contrast between greed and generosity, according to Solomon, is that the greedy individual will be brought ultimately to poverty, while those who give liberally in service to others will be blessed with more to give. Once again, this illustrates that those who insist on trying their own path, rather than God's path, will be disappointed ultimately. God's plan for the use of our blessings is the best plan!

Notice in Proverbs 29:7 that "the righteous considers the cause of the poor." The other verses show us that this is not merely some intellectual or emotional exercise. Rather, their consideration of the poor leads them to act – to do what they can to ease the plight of these less fortunate ones. There must be action involved, not just words (see James 2:15-16).

On the other hand, the wicked one pictured in Proverbs 29:7 is not necessarily actively oppressing the poor – the thought to help the poor just never crosses his mind. This is directly opposite of the attitude displayed by Jesus toward the needy. The Lord was always aware, always compassionate, always caring. That is the same picture that Solomon paints for us in his words about the generosity of the righteous man.

Points to Remember

We should be ready to help others whenever a need arises. If we have managed our finances well, have little or no debt, and have consciously prepared to use our wealth to help others, we will be ready. How ready are we?

There are a number of pressures that work against us when trying to help others. Greed is one such pressure, and it can be a strong one. Solomon's warnings against greed are numerous and plain. God wants us to put others before self, and to trust Him to provide for us. Blessings are promised to those who are willing to distribute to help the needy. Do we believe this? Do our actions demonstrate that we believe it?

Could there be a better investment than lending to the Lord? That is exactly how Solomon describes those who have pity on the poor. God promises to bless those who live lives characterized by generosity.

The New Testament is filled with passages that teach the same lessons Solomon is trying to get across. The Lord's description of the final judgment speaks of the righteous as those who have served the less fortunate (Matthew 25:31-46). The Christians in the young Jerusalem church were almost unbelievably liberal in their giving to support the needy (Acts 4:34-35). Paul repeatedly exhorts the saints to be ready and eager to show their love for others by their generosity (Galatians 6:9-10; Ephesians 4:28; I Timothy 6:17-19). James boils pure religion down to moral purity and service to those in need (James 1:27).

Finally, how can one who claims to follow Christ – the Christ who said "it is more blessed to give than to receive" (Acts 20:35), and who gave His very life for us – greedily hold on to what he has while turning his back on those who desperately need help? We had better find ways to be prepared to help when needs arise!

Chapter 8

Trust God, not riches

*He who trusts in his riches will fall,
but the righteous will flourish like foliage.*

Proverbs 11:28

As we have seen, wealth is a blessing. It is a blessing that God expects us to use in service to Him. Unfortunately, many people begin to put their trust in their wealth. In this chapter, we will see that our trust must be in God, rather than riches. Righteousness before God is what is important – not our material possessions. Solomon refers to striving after wealth as vanity. The lessons in this chapter should help us keep our material possessions, or lack thereof, in the proper perspective.

Trust God Rather Than Riches

The Scriptures teach that there are wealthy people who are pleasing to God, and wealthy people who are not pleasing to God. Obviously, wealth is not the determining factor in one's spiritual condition. The issue that Solomon, and other writers, point to is the heart. As the Lord said in Matthew 6:19-21, "Do not lay up for yourselves treasures on earth, where moth and rust destroy and where thieves break in and steal; but lay up for yourselves treasures in heaven, where neither moth nor rust destroys and where thieves do not break in and steal. For where your treasure is, there your heart will be also."

> The name of the Lord is a strong tower; the righteous run to it and are safe. The rich man's wealth is his strong city, and like a high wall in his own esteem.
> **Proverbs 18:10-11**

> The rich and the poor have this in common, the Lord is the maker of them all.
> **Proverbs 22:2**

> In the day of prosperity be joyful, but in the day of adversity consider: surely God has appointed the one as well as the other, so that man can find out nothing that will come after him.
> **Ecclesiastes 7:14**

> Let us hear the conclusion of the whole matter: fear God and keep His commandments, for this is man's all. For God will bring every work into judgment, including every secret thing, whether good or evil.
>
> Ecclesiastes 12:13-14

God wants His people to look to Him for their strength and protection, rather than trusting in their own strength, wisdom, or wealth. As we have seen, one of the dangers of wealth is pride, which results in self-satisfaction and a failure to rely on God.

Throughout the Old Testament, God tried to get Israel to grasp their dependence on Him, but the lesson went unlearned or forgotten time after time. Even righteous David lapsed in this regard when he numbered his armies, probably a result of his pride at Israel's strength (I Chronicles 21:1-8). God punished David, and Israel, to remind him that God should be our strength, and the only thing in which we glory.

The wealthy are particularly susceptible to this problem of pride, and must be on guard against it always. Consider Paul's words to Timothy:

> Command those who are rich in this present age not to be haughty, nor to trust in uncertain riches but in the living God, who gives us richly all things to enjoy. Let them do good, that they be rich in good works, ready to give, willing to share, storing up for themselves a good foundation for the time to come, that they may lay hold on eternal life.
>
> I Timothy 6:17-19

In the last chapter, we saw how God wants us to use our wealth to help others, and we see Paul making this point to Timothy above. The person who puts his trust in his riches is likely to have a much harder time letting go of some of his wealth to share with others.

Solomon reminds us in Proverbs 22:2 that the rich and the poor have the same Maker. Since God is the Creator of all, all should honor and glorify God. The wealthy man is not any greater in God's eyes than the poor man. Neither is the poor man greater than the wealthy! All should look to God for strength, and place their complete trust in Him – not on anything temporary and material.

God is in control of all things. Any of the plans of man, including his financial plans, can be brought to nothing by the unpredictable fortunes of life, or by the providence of God. Therefore, Solomon tells us that our goal, our aim, our all, should be to honor God and be obedient to Him. We will all be called to account for how well we remember this.

Does the exhortation to trust in God, rather than riches, imply that a Christian should not carry insurance, or have an emergency fund to protect against unexpected events? Some have claimed that taking such steps indicates a lack of trust in God. Certainly, it would be possible to "overdo" in the areas of insurance and emergency funds, and this could result from a failure to trust God sufficiently. However, there are a number of passages in Scripture, including Solomon's writings, which I believe would authorize, and even encourage, such reasonable precautions.

Recall Proverbs 10:15, Ecclesiastes 7:12 and Proverbs 13:7, which speak of money as a protection (see chapter 2); Proverbs 13:22, which speaks favorably of leaving an inheritance (chapter 2); Proverbs 27:23-27, which speaks of the need for diligence in financial management and planning for the future (chapter 5); Ecclesiastes 11:6, which encourages us to do as much as we can to take care of ourselves, while still trusting in God to do for us what we are unable to do (chapter 5); Proverbs 6:6-11, which points to the ant as an example of diligent effort and preparation for the future (chapter 5); and Proverbs 21:5, which says that the plans of the diligent lead to plenty (chapter 5). We could go on to list passages from elsewhere in Scripture, but I believe the point is made. Making reasonable provision for our own, and our family's, financial future shows wisdom, not a lack of trust in God.

Riches and Righteousness Contrasted

God expects His people, whether rich or poor, to live righteously, and to put our trust in Him. Wealth cannot go with us to the grave, and will not help the unrighteous one who faces God's judgment.

> **Riches do not profit in the day of wrath, but righteousness delivers from death.**
> **Proverbs 11:4**
>
> **He who trusts in his riches will fall, but the righteous will flourish like foliage.**
> **Proverbs 11:28**

> There is one who makes himself rich, yet has nothing; and one who makes himself poor, yet has great riches.
>
> Proverbs 13:7

The one who lives a life of faithful service will be delivered from death in the end. There are those who make wealth the goal of their lives, yet they will ultimately have nothing. Those who use their blessings to bless others, even though they may not have as much in this life, will ultimately enjoy all the riches of God's kingdom.

Striving for Wealth is Vanity

Solomon wants us to know that living for God leads to a fulfilling life. Living for material things leads to emptiness. Striving for wealth, he says, is vanity.

> Then I hated all my labor in which I had toiled under the sun, because I must leave it to the man who will come after me. And who knows whether he will be wise or a fool? Yet he will rule over all my labor in which I toiled and in which I have shown myself wise under the sun. This also is vanity. Therefore I turned my heart and despaired of all the labor in which I had toiled under the sun. For there is a man whose labor is with wisdom, knowledge, and skill; yet he must leave his heritage to a man who has not labored for it. This also is vanity and a great evil. For what has man for all his labor, and for the

striving of his heart with which he has toiled under the sun? For all his days are sorrowful, and his work burdensome; even in the night his heart takes no rest. This also is vanity. Nothing is better for a man than that he should eat and drink, and that his soul should enjoy good in his labor. This also, I saw, was from the hand of God. For who can eat, or who can have enjoyment, more than I? For God gives wisdom and knowledge and joy to a man who is good in His sight; but to the sinner He gives the work of gathering and collecting, that he may give to him who is good before God. This also is vanity and grasping for the wind.

Ecclesiastes 2:18-26

We have now looked at all of Solomon's writings that deal with wealth. In this final passage, he strikes a despairing tone to think of the end of a man who would spend his life in a struggle for wealth. What good does this do, ultimately? Solomon's conclusion is that such a life is truly an empty one, without the purpose that the servant of God feels in a life of labor in the Lord's kingdom, with the joys of a life well lived, and the promise of an eternal reward. Which kind of life are you living?

Points to Remember

The righteous have learned to depend on the Lord, rather than on their wealth. Our purpose in life should be to fear God and keep His commandments. That means, of course, that if we are wealthy, we will use that wealth as God directs, in service to Him. God expects us to do what we can to provide for our needs, our family's needs, and the needs of others. This means that making reasonable provisions for the future, including the saving of an emergency fund and the purchase of insurance, represent wise stewardship, rather than a lack of trust in God.

Chapter 9

A financial case study: the virtuous wife

Who can find a virtuous wife? For her worth is far above rubies. The heart of her husband safely trusts her; so he will have no lack of gain.

Proverbs 31:10-11

As we mentioned in the preface, the final two chapters of Proverbs were probably not written by Solomon. The book closes with the unattributed section on the virtuous wife, in Proverbs 31:10-31. Much has been written about this passage, as it presents one of the clearest pictures in Scripture of the character and habits of a virtuous woman.

Our purpose in this chapter is to look at the story of the virtuous wife from a financial perspective. Many of the elements of the financial wisdom of Solomon are demonstrated for us by this unnamed, or hypothetical, woman described here by an unnamed writer. Seeing Solomon's advice applied in this case study should make it easier for us to learn how to apply it in our lives.

The Virtuous Wife is Worth More Than Wealth

We have seen how Solomon makes it clear that wealth is a blessing, but that there are many blessings that are more important than wealth (see chapter 3). In fact, recall that Solomon specifically mentions domestic peace as being better than wealth (see Proverbs 17:1 and 21:9). To have a wife such as the one described here in Proverbs 31 is much more valuable than material wealth.

Who can find a virtuous wife? For her worth is far above rubies. The heart of her husband safely trusts her; so he will have no lack of gain. She does him good and not evil all the days of her life.
Proverbs 31:10-12

Any man who is blessed with a wonderful wife knows how priceless that blessing is. Rubies are valuable because of their beauty, but also because of their rarity. Godly women are characterized by spiritual beauty (see I Peter 3:1-6). Unfortunately, godly women

A Financial Case Study: The Virtuous Wife 103

(and godly men, for that matter) are also far too rare. God's people should work diligently to prepare themselves to be the kind of wives and husbands who will be a blessing to their spouse.

The virtuous wife's husband trusts in her, Solomon says, and this trust is linked to his having no lack of gain. What is the connection between his trust in his wife, and his gain? As we will see when we look further into the passage, she does many things that directly contribute to the financial wellbeing of her family. Beyond that, I believe we see in this passage a real partnership, as God intended marriage to be. The virtuous wife is intelligent and industrious. When financial issues and questions arose in this household, I believe that verse 11 is implying that the husband and wife worked to solve those problems together. The husband would seek, and generally heed, the counsel of his wife. He trusts her advice, and he knows that the family will benefit from her wisdom, including wisdom regarding financial matters.

Think about the way many marriages work, compared to the pattern we have here in Proverbs 31. Remember that money problems are among the leading causes cited as contributing to divorce. There are husbands who fail to include their wives as partners in the financial side of the household. This is not following the Biblical pattern! Recall that Paul said that women are to "manage the house" (I Timothy 5:14). The virtuous wife in Proverbs 31 is a clear illustration of how that can be done. How can a woman manage her house when she is completely shut out of its financial management? Husbands who have approached money matters this way need to repent and follow God's plan for the home!

On the other hand, there are plenty of women who have not prepared themselves to contribute in a meaningful way to the financial management of the home. Worse yet, there are women who seem to view their role as that of spending the money faster than it comes in. These women also need to repent, show fiscal restraint themselves, and learn to work with their husbands to ensure that they are acting as good stewards of the financial blessings they have. A wife needs to be ready to do her husband "good and not evil all the days of her life," in every aspect of life, including finances.

The Virtuous Wife Works Hard and Intelligently

As we noted in chapter 5, Solomon has a lot to say about the need for hard work, and the connection between hard work and financial blessings. It is not surprising that the virtuous wife is described, at some length, as an industrious and intelligent woman, whose diligent effort reaps benefits for her family, as well as for others to whom she gives assistance. Notice all of the different ways that she makes herself busy working for the benefit of others.

> She seeks wool and flax, and willingly works with her hands. She is like the merchant ships, she brings her food from afar. She also rises while it is yet night, and provides food for her household, and a portion for her

A Financial Case Study: The Virtuous Wife

maidservants. She considers a field and buys it; from her profits she plants a vineyard. She girds herself with strength, and strengthens her arms. She perceives that her merchandise is good, and her lamp does not go out by night. She stretches out her hands to the distaff, and her hand holds the spindle.

Proverbs 31:13-19

She makes linen garments and sells them, and supplies sashes for the merchants.

Proverbs 31:24

She watches over the ways of her household, and does not eat the bread of idleness.

Proverbs 31:27

The virtuous wife works hard to provide for herself, for her family, and for others. She works willingly, and at a variety of tasks. Notice the diversification of her efforts: (1) she does manual labor, (2) she is a diligent bargain-hunter, using her financial resources wisely, (3) she provides food for her household and her servants, (4) she shows an entrepreneurial spirit by buying real estate and acquiring and managing a vineyard, (5) she sells the garments that she makes with her own hands, and (6) she watches over the ways of her household.

Most women – and most men, for that matter – will not necessarily be involved in this many different types of financial activity, but the illustration is strong and clear. This woman is characterized by diligent effort and intelligence, aimed at providing a better life for herself, her family, and others whom she can serve. The wife who searches for bargains in the stores or at garage sales, who clips coupons, who looks for ways to supplement the household income, or who stretches the household budget in other ways, is certainly following the pattern left for us by the virtuous wife of Proverbs 31.

Although the story of the virtuous wife is sometimes used as a defense of women working at an outside career, I believe that is not the point. There is plenty of work for Christian women to be doing, and women who choose to work at home can, and should, stay busy working for others, and for the Lord. Young (or older) women who feel as if they would be bored without a job outside the home need to get some wisdom in this regard. There are plenty of women who understand how to stay busy while working at home. If you wonder how they do it, ask them! I do not believe the virtuous wife had what we would typically refer to as a career, but she certainly was a working woman.

The Virtuous Wife Knows How to Use Wealth

Wealth is a blessing that we are expected to manage carefully and use properly. The virtuous wife obviously realized that. She used some wealth for herself, but was most concerned with providing for her family and helping others.

A Financial Case Study: The Virtuous Wife

> She extends her hand to the poor, yes, she reaches out her hands to the needy. She is not afraid of snow for her household, for all her household is clothed with scarlet. She makes tapestry for herself; her clothing is fine linen and purple.
>
> Proverbs 31:20-22

The virtuous wife is ever aware of the plight of the poor, and does what she can to help them. She knows that one of the main purposes of wealth for the godly person is to share with the needy (see I Timothy 6:17-19, for example). There is no hint of selfishness in her.

The hard work of the wife has allowed her to provide for her family. They are well clothed and well fed, and thus are prepared for difficult times that may arise. Her family trusts in her, just as she trusts in God.

Finally, we see in verse 22 that the virtuous woman understands that God wants His people to enjoy the fruits of their labor. After providing for her family and serving others, she uses some of her wealth to provide comforts – even luxuries – for herself. As we have seen, Solomon (and God) would approve of this.

The Virtuous Wife is a Blessing

The virtuous wife is a blessing for her husband, for her children, and for many others whose lives she touches. God approves of her life, and wants us to learn these lessons from her wisdom.

> Her children rise up and call her blessed; her husband also, and he praises her: "Many daughters have done well, but you excel them all." Charm is deceitful and beauty is passing, but a woman who fears the Lord, she shall be praised. Give her of the fruit of her hands, and let her own works praise her in the gates.
>
> Proverbs 31:28-31

This righteous woman has, with her diligence, intelligence, and love for her family and for others, earned their love and respect in return. Her loved ones appreciate her, and are thankful for the blessings she brings to their lives. Seeing such a godly individual should help us see the wisdom in God's plan. Yes, she has wealth, but her life is a graphic demonstration of the fact that "a good name is to be chosen rather than great riches" (Proverbs 22:1).

We need to be praying that more virtuous women will arise in our society to show the wisdom of God's plan. But we need to be doing more than praying. Women need to be working to make themselves more virtuous. Parents need to be teaching their daughters God's plan for them. One of the lessons of this passage is that one godly woman can have a tremendous positive impact on God's kingdom, and on the world. The

A Financial Case Study: The Virtuous Wife

next time you see a virtuous woman, thank her for the good work she is doing, and "praise her in the gates."

Points to Remember

The story of the virtuous wife shows us that the work of godly women is vitally important. When we think about this story from a financial perspective, we see clearly the value of hard work. The work of the wife is essential to the family's financial wellbeing. Rather than keeping his wife in the dark regarding money matters, the picture here is of a husband who depends heavily on the wisdom and hard work of his wife.

The virtuous wife is wise enough to follow God's plan for wealth. She sees her wealth as a blessing from God, which is to be used in serving Him. She knows that God wants her to provide for the needs of her family, and to share with others. She is mindful of the needy, because she knows that God is always mindful of them. She does not close her eyes to the poor and wait for the government, or anyone else, to take care of them. She unselfishly does what she can with what she has. Finally, she knows that God is pleased when His people enjoy the fruits of their labors, as long as they are putting Him, and others, before themselves.

Chapter 10

Transform your life

*Let us hear the conclusion of the whole matter:
Fear God and keep His commandments, for this is man's all.*

Ecclesiastes 12:13

Solomon has given us a great deal of wisdom about wealth. It is up to us to decide what to do with this information. Each of us needs to ask ourselves if we are really following God's plans for our finances. God's plans work. We may not like them. They may be painful. We can choose to ignore them if we want to. Most people will ignore them. If we choose to follow God's plans, we will always be better off in the long run, and we will usually be better off in the short run, as well.

Solomon told us something about the attitude we need to have toward wealth. Wealth is a blessing from God, but it is not the most important blessing. Wealth is also a danger. We may need to transform our attitudes to match God's plan. If we have the proper attitude toward wealth, we will act differently. Solomon gives some specific instructions on how we should act in financial matters. He tells us to work diligently, to avoid debt, to help others, and to trust God, not riches.

This is not meant to be a theoretical book, just as Solomon did not mean for his instructions to be merely theoretical. In this chapter, we will attempt to give some very practical suggestions, based directly on the wisdom of Solomon, for helping us to transform our lives in regard to our finances. Finding ways to implement Solomon's financial wisdom in our lives will bless us as God intends for His people to be blessed.

Transforming Our Attitude Toward Wealth: Seeing Wealth as a Blessing

We need to see wealth as God sees it. Hopefully, spending time reading Solomon's thoughts on wealth has helped us do that. To reinforce the proper attitudes toward wealth, consider the following questions:

1. Would it be a blessing if you had more money to give to God?
2. Would it be a blessing if you had more money to help a struggling single mother?
3. Would it be a blessing if you had more money to help a widow?
4. Would it be a blessing if you had more money to help support a missionary?

5. Would it be a blessing if you had more money to help send an underprivileged child to college?
6. Would it be a blessing if you had more money to expand your business and employ more people?
7. Would it be a blessing if you had more money to help pay off the mortgage on a church building?
8. Would it be a blessing if you had more money to help when a medical emergency struck a friend or relative?
9. Would it be a blessing if you had more money to contribute to a worthy charity helping victims of a natural disaster?
10. Would it be a blessing if you had more money so that you could help a needy person who asked you for assistance?
11. Would it be a blessing if you had more money to comfortably care for your aged parents or grandparents?
12. Would it be a blessing if you had more money so that you had less worry in your life?
13. Would it be a blessing if you had more money so you could be debt free?
14. Would it be a blessing if you had more money so your family could live in a nice (I did *not* say "extravagant") home?
15. Would it be a blessing if you had more money so you could take your family on a nice (I did *not* say "extravagant") vacation each year?

Based on what Solomon wrote, I believe he would answer all of the above questions affirmatively. We certainly need to be careful about some of the actions implied in the fifteen questions (for example, Paul teaches us in II Thessalonians 3:10 that we should not encourage someone's laziness), but the Scriptures support the idea that all the actions in these fifteen questions are approved actions. This means that having more money so that we can accomplish these actions would be a blessing. Wealth becomes a problem for us when we either make it an end in itself, rather than a means to a good end, or when we use it in ways that God would disapprove.

In chapter two, we discussed six approved ways to use wealth. These include (1) honoring God with our firstfruits, (2) providing needed sustenance, (3) providing financial security and protection, (4) providing for one's family, including through inheritances, (5) enjoying, and (6) sharing with others. Seeing wealth as a blessing will lead us to want to manage our wealth properly, which will mean that we would want to plan carefully in order to properly prioritize the different uses of wealth. We will discuss some practical aspects of sound financial management in more detail in a later section.

Transforming Our Attitude Toward Wealth: The Christian and Workaholism

Solomon says quite a lot about what we call workaholism, and he clearly disapproves of it. Nevertheless, this continues to be a problem for many who profess to be serving God. Since the Scriptures are so clear on this, the problem must be one of *behavior*, rather than *knowledge*.

Self-examination is obviously an important step here. We first need to ask ourselves if we have a tendency toward workaholism, and we should realize that we may be unlikely to see our situation objectively and accurately. Therefore, we may need to ask others if they see this tendency in us. If we find that we may have a problem, then we have to devise a plan to combat it.

Here is one suggestion. Make a list of half a dozen activities that (1) have nothing to do with your job, (2) focus on being with and/or helping others, and (3) could fill up one day. Then, for the next six months, take one day off work each month to do the things you have listed. Take your family on a picnic. Take your children fishing. Spend a day with your family doing yard work for a widow. Take a day trip with your spouse. Spend the day with your parents. Visit an old friend whom you have not seen in years. Use your imagination! At the end of each of these days off, write down in a journal some brief thoughts on that day. At the end of the six-month period, review your journal entries, and then ask yourself whether these days were more, or less, fulfilling than a day at work. Then maybe try it for another six months. Who knows? You may create a new habit, find yourself more able to keep work in perspective, grow closer to your family, and be less inclined to be self-centered.

Transforming Our Attitude Toward Wealth: Proper Use of a Financial Windfall

In chapter four, we looked at some of the dangers that can come with wealth. Greed is one of those dangers, and it takes on many forms. One indicator of our attitude toward wealth may be the way we use a financial windfall. Remember that, in Proverbs 25:16, Solomon says, "Have you found honey? Eat only as much as you need, lest you be filled with it and vomit." Try to recall a recent occasion where you received an unexpected or unusual sum of money – a gift, wages from an extra job or overtime, contest winnings, even an income tax refund. How did you view that money? How did you use it?

If we don't plan for the use of a windfall, there is a danger that we will use it in an unwise, or even selfish, manner. Does it occur to you to give some of this money to help others, or does it all become "blow" money? Proverbs 25:16 is addressing this situation, and we need to pay attention.

Here is a suggested general plan for the use of a windfall. It is, again, a *suggestion*, but I believe it is based on principles we see in the Scriptures. Modify the plan as you see fit, but *develop and use some plan!*

First, divide the money into at least three (unequal) parts: (1) firstfruits and sharing, (2) wealth building (including debt reduction), and (3) enjoying. These categories are approved uses for our money. Now you will need to think about appropriate portions of the money for each of the categories.

The firstfruits of our increase should always be given to God. What portion of a windfall should be given? That is, of course, a personal decision, but let me suggest a plan. Consider taking the percentage you give of your normal income, and doubling that percentage. Again, this is just a suggestion, but think about what this will do. It will help you to remember that all your wealth comes from, and, in fact, belongs to God. This windfall is, by definition, unexpected increase. Since you were not dependent on it or planning on it, you should be able to give more of it up. View this windfall as an *opportunity* to give back to God, rather than as a *duty*. If you are in a solid financial position, consider including an even higher percentage here.

The windfall is an unusual opportunity for you to be of service directly to others, in addition to contributions you may make to your church. Send some of the money to a missionary family, help a needy person in your neighborhood, or put some money aside in your "benevolence envelope" (more on that later) to be available when an opportunity arises. Again, if you are in a solid financial position, consider including a higher percentage here.

Under "wealth building" in the second portion, I would include saving or investing for the future, or paying off debt. The suggested amount to be allocated here would depend greatly on your current financial situation. If you have significant debt, Solomon's instructions would indicate that removing that debt is of high priority, so you would want a large portion to be paid on the debt. In fact, if we look again at what Elisha told the widow to do with the proceeds from the miraculously-produced oil (II Kings 4:7), we see that he put paying off her debts as the first priority. If you have little or no debt and are already saving, say, 10-15% of your income, then you would want to save at least that portion of your windfall, and probably somewhat more than that.

Finally, there is the portion that you use for enjoyment. It is no accident that this plan has put this part last. As we have seen, using wealth for our own enjoyment is perfectly acceptable, according to Solomon. However, this is not the primary use we are to make of our money. Putting ourselves last seems to mesh quite nicely with the Biblical model. If you have debts, this portion should be quite small.

To review these suggestions, consider, just for an example, someone who normally gives ten percent as a regular offering. The guidelines above would yield something like the following two allocations of a windfall for someone with significant debt, versus someone without debt:

Category	With Debt	No Debt
Offering/Sharing	20%	40%
Wealth Building	70% (debt)	30%
Enjoying	10%	30%

Let me repeat yet again that this is merely an example. It is presented just to illustrate one approach that is, I believe, based on the Biblical principles we have learned from Solomon. The basic lesson from Proverbs 25:16 is that we need to think about how to use a windfall appropriately – in service to God – rather than blowing it all on ourselves.

Transforming Our Behavior: Diligent Financial Management

Many Christians fail to be good stewards of their financial blessings, not because of greed, but simply because of inattention in the area of financial management. One common reason for such inattention is simple laziness. If there is one lesson we should have learned from Solomon it is this: *there is no excuse for laziness!* If laziness has characterized your financial management practices, you need to first face your problem and *repent*. Repentance means a change of heart, and true repentance is followed by a change of behavior. The time has come to "be diligent to know the state of your flocks, and attend to your herds" (Proverbs 27:23).

Not everyone who has failed to be diligent with financial affairs is guilty of laziness. Suppose that a young couple has decided that one of them will be responsible for most of the household financial management. Perhaps the husband assigns this task to his stay-at-home wife. In many instances, the wife may feel enormous pressure as a result of this task, and feel as if her husband needs to participate more. The husband, however, is busy with a new job, and does not really realize all of the burdens his wife is facing at home, particularly if there are small children in the house. The wife struggles on alone with the finances, has trouble keeping up with the job, fails in her efforts to get her husband more involved, becomes increasingly frustrated, and finally just "gives up." The credit card balances begin to increase, and the spiral toward major financial problems begins. When the problems become severe, the husband can no longer ignore them, and asks his wife the inevitable question, "What happened?", or maybe even the cruel question, "What have you been doing?"

Husbands and wives need to communicate, regularly and significantly, about finances. If your spouse is asking for more help and discussion with financial matters, you should view this as a serious warning sign. Pay attention. Be more involved. Learn to work together and support one another in this vital area of life. A family's financial assets are blessings to both the husband and wife, and both are responsible for good stewardship.

This does not mean, of course, that the husband and wife are necessarily equally involved in all financial tasks, but some involvement is necessary for both, and communication is absolutely essential to effective financial management. There are countless stories of financial counselors working with widows who have been left with little or no knowledge of the family's financial situation. This should never happen!

Financial management involves both planning and control. Financial planning involves budgeting (or "cash flow planning," or "spending planning," if you prefer). Most people try to follow a financial plan. They typically find it relatively easy to *develop* the plan. They often find it extremely difficult to *follow* the plan. (That's the "control" part of financial management).

There are numerous good books on financial management, including many that are written from a Biblical perspective. In Appendix 2, you will find brief reviews of some books that you may want to consider reading to increase your basic financial knowledge, as well as to help provide the motivation you will need to keep applying good financial management principles over the long run.

The best planning and control mechanisms I have seen can be found in Dave Ramsey's *The Total Money Makeover*.[1] You need to get this book and read it. The real beauty of these approaches is in their simplicity, which is critical in making financial management workable. I will give a very brief summary of these planning and control approaches here, and refer you to Mr. Ramsey's book for the details.

I would highly recommend that you consider budgeting by *pay period*, rather than by month, for those who are not paid monthly. Many people struggle with budgeting because their budgets just never seem to work. In some cases, this is probably because they develop a budget for the *average* month, but then the average month never happens. They become frustrated when they can't meet their budget, and finally just give up on budgeting. Planning by pay period should help solve some of this frustration. Of course, if budgeting on a monthly basis works well for you, keep doing it that way!

A day or two before each payday (or the end of the month, if you are budgeting monthly), the plan for the next pay period should be developed. Dave Ramsey suggests that you "spend every dollar on paper." In other words, use the budget forms such as those in *The Total Money Makeover* to allocate every dollar of the coming paycheck to the specific expense items. This gives you a very detailed plan for spending your money. The forms provide a very comprehensive list of likely spending categories, and you should, of course, modify them to fit your situation, as needed.

Every dollar should be spent on paper. If there is money left over when all necessary expenses are satisfied, then that money should be allocated somewhere – to savings, investments, gifts, "blow" money – it has to be assigned. On the other hand, if there is a deficit, then allocated funds in some categories must be reduced until the budget balances. After all, none of us can print money like the government can!

Having this detailed spending plan is a critical first step in sound financial management, but then comes the hard part. You have to find a way to make the plan work. Many personal finance professionals recommend the "envelope system" as a simple, yet incredibly effective mechanism for implementing the control aspect of a financial management system. Probably no one knows how long the envelope system has been around, but it is just as effective today as it was when our grandparents and great-grandparents used it. Don't make the mistake of scoffing at simple, low-tech solutions. Engineers often refer to simple, yet effective, solutions as "elegant" solutions, and the envelope system is definitely in that category.

You can build an envelope-based system for financial control around as few as about half a dozen envelopes for key spending categories where discipline is hardest to maintain. For example, you might choose to use envelopes only for groceries, eating out, gasoline, clothing, and entertainment. Since these categories account for much of the discretionary spending in most households, if you do a good job of controlling them, your entire financial situation will tend to be in control.

Discipline is the key to making a financial plan work, and the envelope system helps to impose discipline. If there is no money left in the envelope, then you cannot purchase anything else in that category during that pay period, unless you choose to move money from another category. Many people find the idea of limiting expenditures so tightly like this to be repugnant. Typically, those people are *not* living on what they make, and don't really want to.

Remember, *you* are "giving every dollar a name" in advance, so *you* are determining how much to allocate to each category and/or envelope. As an aside, you should realize that every time you take on a debt, you commit to repaying that debt as agreed, so the minimum payments on those credit cards must be made. By incurring the debt, you just surrendered that much of the control of your finances to your creditor. Truly, the borrower is slave to the lender!

Transforming Our Behavior: Avoiding (and Escaping) Debt

Remember the bottom line of our discussion in chapter 6 was that the Scriptures *never* speak favorably of debt. Debt was actually pictured in the Old Testament as a curse on those who failed to follow God. If we change our attitude toward debt and view it as an inherently undesirable thing, our behavior toward debt should follow that change in attitude. Saving to build up an emergency fund will remove much of the "need" for borrowing. Many financial advisors recommend an emergency fund of three to six months' worth of expenses. Whether you choose to use the lower figure or higher figure is largely a function of factors such as the stability of your job situation, your health, and the size of your family. Saving for this purpose is simply sound financial planning, and should help remove reliance on borrowed money, particularly credit card debt. You should always be careful to use the emergency fund for real emergencies, rather than for expenses you should have planned for, but didn't. Also, when you have to tap into the emergency fund, you should make replenishing the fund as soon as possible a high priority.

Many financial advisors recommend paying off debts in order of highest interest rate first, and this is certainly a reasonable approach. However, Larry Burkett, Dave Ramsey, and others, recommend using "the debt snowball" to escape from debt. This involves listing the debts in order of smallest dollar amount first. After the smallest debt is paid off, that monthly payment amount is added to the payments on the next smallest, and so on. The debt reduction payments grow larger and larger as the small debts are paid off. Psychologically, this approach provides powerful positive feedback and momentum. Since most people struggle with financial discipline, the debt snowball approach may actually work better for them.

It was noted in chapter 6 that there are several reasons why people incur debt, including (1) greed, (2) failure to plan for the future, (3) careless financial management, or (4) an unforeseeable catastrophic event. If you face significant debt, I would recommend doing some careful soul-searching regarding the reason for the debt. Being honest with yourself about the cause of your debts is an important step toward stopping the accumulation of debt and working on a plan to repay the debts you have.

Finally, I would suggest that you sit down with your financial data and envision how your circumstances would change if your debt were gone. To illustrate the possible impact, consider the following facts:

- The median household income in the U.S. for the period 2002 – 2004 was $44,473.[2] (This would result in a monthly take-home pay of approximately $3,000).
- The average American household with at least one credit card has $8,523 in credit card debt, at an average annual interest rate of 14.4%.[3] (This would result in a minimum monthly payment of around $150, including monthly interest charges of about $102).
- The average monthly car payment for new cars sold in October 2003 was $447, with an average financing period of more than 62 months, and an average annual interest rate of 5.63%.[4]

If a "typical" family, as represented by the above statistics, eliminated their credit card debt, this would free up $150 per month, which is 5% of their take-home pay. If they eliminated a $447 monthly car payment by, for example, paying cash for a used car, this would free up almost another 15% of their net income. Taking this $597 per month and earning interest on it, rather than paying interest, would dramatically improve this family's circumstance. In addition to relieving them of the strain associated with the debt, they could use the money previously needed for interest payments to save for a car, college, or other future needs, or they could increase their charitable giving or pay their home off early.

I would encourage you to examine your own financial circumstances from this perspective to see what the effects of eliminating your debt might be. In order to become free of debt, you need to believe that it is possible, develop a plan for making it happen, and then have the discipline to stay with that plan. I believe Solomon is encouraging us to give this a try!

Transforming Our Behavior: Helping Others

Solomon says that having pity on the poor is like lending to the Lord. Christians are to be giving people. Unfortunately, many of us have difficulty in this area. Often, the difficulties arise not because we are greedy or selfish (if those are our problems, we need to repent), but because we do not have our finances in order such that we can share significantly with others. If we follow God's plan of hard work, diligent financial management, and avoiding debt, we should be in a position to help others, just as we saw the virtuous wife doing.

Christians have an individual responsibility to share with others (see, for example, Ephesians 4:28 and I Timothy 6:17-19). Putting money in the collection plate – even a generous amount – does not relieve us of our responsibility to help others. On the other hand, I do not think we should have to borrow money to give to others in normal circumstances (remember Solomon's instructions on surety). I would conclude, then, that we are going to have to do some planning in the area of sharing.

To plan effectively for benevolence, we are going to have to have a line item for it in our budget. Some control has to be exercised, also, or we may put our own family's financial situation at risk due to our propensity to give to every needy cause or person who asks us for help. The stronger our giving nature becomes, the more of a problem this might be. The envelope system can be used quite effectively in this situation. The "benevolence" or "sharing" envelope can be funded regularly, just like the grocery and clothing envelopes, so that money is readily available as opportunities for sharing arise. If the envelope is empty, then that signals that we may have to wait to support the giving opportunity or, in critical cases, move money from other categories into the sharing fund. By the way, taking money out of your grocery envelope to share with a needy person presents a great opportunity to teach your children about sacrificial giving.

In Ephesians 4:28, Paul says that giving to others is one of the primary reasons that we work. No matter what method you choose to use for sharing your wealth, it is an opportunity for serving that we must not ignore. Following God's total plan for wealth will make it much easier for us to serve in this way.

Transforming Our Behavior:
Trusting God, Not Riches

As we noted in chapter 8, Solomon's instructions to trust God, rather than wealth, would not preclude us from making provisions for our future. In fact, building an emergency fund and purchasing insurance are important parts of a reasonable and diligent financial plan. No matter how much we prepare, it is possible that a financial catastrophe may strike that causes us to have to turn to others for help. Those who are truly needy, through no fault of their own, have nothing to be ashamed of, and should not refuse the help of others who are trying to practice "pure and undefiled religion" (see James 1:27). However, those who fail to plan for the future have certainly not learned the lesson of the ant (Proverbs 6:6-11).

There is a tremendous amount of good information available on long-term financial planning, including insurance needs. *The World's Easiest Guide to Finances*, by Larry Burkett, and *Master Your Money*, by Ron Blue, (both listed in Appendix 2) provide comprehensive discussions of the various types of insurance you may need to consider, and how to determine your needs. If you are not prepared for the future, start working on that immediately. Buy or borrow a good book or ask a friend for help, but don't continue to put this off – that is irresponsible!

There is a big difference between planning for your future, which God directs that His people *should* do, and being consumed with worry about your future, which God directs that His people *must not* do. If I think my insurance policies and investments can protect me from any problems I may face, I am (1) naïve or stupid, and (2) guilty of trusting in my wealth. My trust must be in God. Fearing Him and keeping His commandments must be my primary concerns.

Points to Remember

Solomon's wisdom on wealth, as on many other areas, is both profound and simple. In His writings, we see God's plan for our finances laid out for us. God wants us to see that wealth is a blessing, but that it is not the most important blessing God gives us, and can, in fact, be a danger if we do not handle it properly. We are to work hard and practice diligent financial management. We should try to avoid debt. One of the most important uses for our wealth is to help others. Finally, we are to always put our trust in God, rather than in our money.

Hopefully, we have learned a lot about what God would want us to do regarding money. The hard part comes in making ourselves change our behavior. In this chapter, we have seen some of the attitude changes that we may need to make, and I have made some suggestions on how to implement Solomon's instructions. In Appendix 3, I have listed some specific steps you may want to take to get started in the right direction. If you don't like my suggestions, that's fine, but find some way to put Solomon's teachings into practice in your life. The books listed in Appendix 2 can help you find out more about managing your money with a Biblical perspective. Read, learn, and be diligent about using your money as God would want. We cannot afford to ignore God's plan for our finances!

Finally, never forget that – as the Lord Himself said in Matthew 6:21 – "where your treasure is, there your heart will be also." I hope this book will help encourage you to do a better job of remembering where our treasure must be, while learning more about how to please God with those things he has entrusted to our care.

Appendix 1

Proverbs 30 and 31 on wealth

Give me neither poverty nor riches – feed me with the food allotted to me; lest I be full and deny You, and say, "Who is the Lord?" or lest I be poor and steal, and profane the name of my God.

Proverbs 30:8-9

As we noted in the preface, most Biblical scholars believe that chapters 30 and 31 of Proverbs were probably not written by Solomon. The story of the virtuous wife from Proverbs 31 has been used as the basis of chapter 9. For the sake of completeness, we are including a brief discussion of the other wealth-related passages from Proverbs 30 and 31 in this appendix. The thrust of these passages serves primarily to reinforce the main ideas from Solomon's writing.

Both Wealth and Poverty are Dangerous

> Remove falsehood and lies far from me; give me neither poverty nor riches – feed me with the food allotted to me; lest I be full and deny You, and say "Who is the Lord?" or lest I be poor and steal, and profane the name of my God.
>
> Proverbs 30:8-9

As we discussed at some length in chapter four, wealth is a danger. This passage points out one of the dangers associated with great riches – the temptation to forget God. The passage also points out one of the dangers associated with severe poverty – the temptation to resort to sinful means to gain wealth, and thereby dishonor God.

Both rich and poor people can faithfully serve God. I do not believe that the point of the passage is that God's children should strive to be "middle class" economically. Note the prayer to "feed me with the food allotted to me." This indicates an attitude of willingness to accept whatever personal circumstances fit God's plan. This is the same attitude Paul expressed in Philippians 4:11-13 when he said, "... I have learned in whatever state I am, to be content: I know how to be abased, and I know how to abound. Everywhere and in all things I have learned both to be full and to be hungry, both to abound and to suffer need. I can do all things through Christ who strengthens me."

The child of God is to be a contented individual. This is not to say that Christians are to be self-satisfied, complacent, lacking in ambition, or lazy. The person who truly trusts in God, and is ever aware of the dangers facing them in their given circumstance in life, can find a way to "do all things through Christ."

Wealth Often Leads to Pride

> For three things the earth is perturbed, yes, for four it cannot bear up: for a servant when he reigns, a fool when he is filled with food, a hateful woman when she is married, and a maidservant who succeeds her mistress.
> Proverbs 30:21-23

The author presents four incongruities here. All involve situations where someone is elevated suddenly to a higher station or circumstance in life. Such situations often – but not always – result in the person being lifted up with pride and self-importance. Most people are turned off by those who are full of themselves. More importantly, the proud make themselves an abomination in God's eyes (Proverbs 6:16-19). That should be all the warning we need to try and avoid pride at all costs.

Solomon on Wealth

Poverty Can Lead to Misery

> It is not for kings, O Lemuel, it is not for kings to drink wine, nor for princes intoxicating drink; lest they drink and forget the law, and pervert the justice of all the afflicted. Give strong drink to him who is perishing, and wine to those who are bitter of heart. Let him drink and forget his poverty, and remember his misery no more.
> Proverbs 31:4-7

David spoke of the blessings of wine, oil, and bread in improving a man's physical and emotional well-being (Psalm 104:14-15). Wine was often used in ancient times for medicinal and restorative purposes. Our primary interest in this passage is in the fact that a man's poverty could place him in a state of mental and physical misery and depression. When someone is so poor that his life is a constant struggle for subsistence, it is difficult for him to maintain a calm and peaceful outlook. God intends for his people to find enjoyment in the physical blessings of life, while understanding that these blessings are not to be what gives primary meaning to our lives. How much better it is to have enough of life's blessings to enjoy and share with others, rather than to turn to some "escape" from a life of constant misery!

Do Not Oppress the Poor

> There is a generation whose teeth are like swords, and whose fangs are like knives, to devour the poor from off the earth, and the needy from among men.
>
> Proverbs 30:14

As we saw in chapter 4, Solomon had quite a lot to say to warn the rich against ill treatment of the poor. He warned in Proverbs 22:22-23 that the Lord will plead the cause of the poor and afflicted, and will plunder the soul of those who oppress them. Anyone who would take advantage of the poor is truly abominable in God's eyes.

Work Hard and Plan for the Future

> There are four things which are little on the earth, but they are exceedingly wise: the ants are a people not strong, yet they prepare their food in the summer; the rock badgers are a feeble folk, yet they make their homes in the crags; the locusts have no king, yet they all advance in ranks; the spider skillfully grasps with its hands, and it is in kings' palaces.
>
> Proverbs 30:24-28

The ants are said to be wise because they prepare for the future. It shows wisdom when God's people prepare adequately for their futures by taking steps such as saving for retirement, buying insurance, and preparing wills or trusts. To ignore such provisions for the future is not, as some teach, a sign of trust in God; rather, it is folly.

Take Opportunities to Help Others

Open your mouth for the speechless, in the cause of all who are appointed to die. Open your mouth, judge righteously, and plead the cause of the poor and needy.
                                                          Proverbs 31:8-9

Children of God should want to be in a position where they are able to help others. Rather than taking advantage of the poor, as many do, God's people should have compassion and concern for the needy that moves them to act to relieve their suffering as they have opportunities to do so. James expresses a similar thought when he says that, "Pure and undefiled religion before God and the Father is this: to visit orphans and widows in their trouble, and to keep oneself unspotted from the world." (James 1:27).

Appendix 2

Financial books with a Biblical perspective

Brief reviews are presented below for some books that have influenced my study and personal financial habits. Since motivation is such a key factor in effective financial management, I strongly recommend that you read books such as the ones listed here to learn more about the practical side of using money effectively.

With one notable exception, these books look at financial matters from a Biblical perspective. The exception is George S. Clason's *The Richest Man in Babylon*. I believe Christians will enjoy Clason's classic, and can gain much from it, even though they should realize that "pay yourself first" is not quite right!

The books are presented in alphabetical order by author's last name.

Blomberg, Craig L., *Heart, Soul, and Money,* **College Press Publishing Company, Joplin, Missouri, 2000, 111 pages.**

Designed as a study guide with questions after each of the nine chapters, Blomberg's book provides an excellent overview of what the Bible has to say about money. Although obviously not an exhaustive study, the book captures most of the key financial concepts in Scripture. In the book's concluding chapter, the author lists the following five most important conclusions of the study: (1) material possessions are a gift from God, (2) material possessions are also one of the primary means of turning hearts away from God, (3) redeemed individuals should be transformed in the area of stewardship, (4) extremes of both wealth and poverty can be intolerable, and (5) scriptural teachings on material possessions are inextricably linked with more "spiritual" matters such as love, faith, and trust.

Blue, Ron, *Master Your Money*, Revised and Updated Edition, Thomas Nelson Publishers, Nashville, Tennessee, 1997, 227 pages.

This book covers the attitudes that God's people should have toward money, as well as the practical issues that we face when dealing with money on a daily basis. The book starts by setting forth some basic principles of money management to show the importance of proper stewardship of God's blessings to us. With these foundational principles in place, it moves into discussions of the need for personal financial planning, the importance of saving, the dangers of debt, common financial mistakes, taxes, investing, wills/trusts, and charitable giving. Numerous examples and worksheets are presented to help explain the concepts.

Burkett, Larry, *Business by the Book*, Updated Edition, Thomas Nelson Publishers, Nashville, Tennessee, 1998, 256 pages.

This is a very practical guide for individuals who are interested in managing their lives, and especially their businesses, by Biblical principles. Mr. Burkett attempts to capture the rules by which God would have his people manage their work lives. He includes discussion of what the Bible says that relates to hiring and firing decisions, employee rewards and discipline, employee selection, business borrowing and lending, and the formation of corporations and partnerships.

Financial Books with a Biblical Perspective 139

Burkett, Larry, *Debt-Free Living,* **Moody Press, Chicago, Illinois, 1999, 232 pages.**
As its subtitle suggests, this book is about "how to get out of debt and stay out." It begins with a look at realistic examples of how people fall into debt. The next major section details how to escape from debt, and how to remain debt-free. An overview of most important debt-related topics is presented, including a discussion of the different types of debt, ideas on dealing with creditors, how to live with bankruptcy, and how to find help with debt-related problems. The book contains an excellent presentation of what the Bible has to say about debt and borrowing.

Burkett, Larry, with Randy Southern, *"The World's Easiest Guide" to Finances,* **Northfield Publishing, Chicago, Illinois, 2000, 409 pages.**
This is a clear, yet comprehensive, manual covering most of the important issues related to personal finance. It contains detailed discussions of debt, budgeting, making major purchases, investments, retirement planning, insurance, wills and trusts, special advice for various family situations such as single living and college planning, and financial attitudes and values. Numerous useful worksheets are included in the appendix. Though it is clearly written from Biblical principles, this is subtly done such that it should be well-received by your non-Christian friends, as well.

Clason, George S., *The Richest Man in Babylon,* **Signet: Penguin Putnam Books, New York, New York, 1926, 144 pages.**
This is certainly one of the most famous motivational books on personal finance ever written, as well as one of the best. Although it is not written from a Biblical perspective, most Bible students will enjoy this book of parables set in ancient Babylon. The richest man in Babylon shares his financial wisdom with his friends, including his seven cures for a lean purse and the five laws of gold. This is a book that should be read as a teenager, and then re-read every few years thereafter.

Dayton, Howard, *Your Money Counts,* **Tyndale House Publishers, Carol Stream, Illinois, 1996, 169 pages.**

Dayton (co-founder, with Larry Burkett, of Crown Financial Ministries) provides a comprehensive look at what it means to be a faithful steward of material blessings. Using faithful stewardship as a unifying concept, Dayton discusses work, spending, investing, giving, debt, honesty, and other key issues related to finances. The book is filled with references to scripture, and provides clear contrasts between what society often says about financial issues and what the Bible says. This book provides an excellent foundation for developing a Biblical perspective of wealth.

Getz, Gene, *Rich in Every Way,* **Howard Publishing, West Monroe, Louisiana, 2004, 346 pages.**

Dr. Gene Getz presents a detailed examination of all the scriptural teachings on wealth. This book is the outgrowth of a study by the author and others, which was aimed at finding out all the Bible has to say about money and possessions. The book concludes with 102 Biblical principles for handling material possessions. Although Old Testament passages were included in the study, the primary focus was on the New Testament. This is an excellent resource for anyone wishing to understand what the Bible has to say about wealth.

Ramsey, Dave, *Financial Peace Revisited,* **Viking: Penguin Putnam Books, New York, New York, 2003, 319 pages.**

This is the revised version of the financial counselor and talk show host's first best selling book. He focuses on the behavioral aspects of dealing with finances while discussing a wide range of personal financial management issues from making career choices to the effects of finances on your marriage. As in all his books, Ramsey emphasizes the importance of debt-free living on achieving and maintaining financial peace. The relationship between proper financial management and a healthy spiritual life is highlighted. Many easy-to-use financial management worksheets are included.

Financial Books with a Biblical Perspective

Ramsey, Dave, *More Than Enough,* **Penguin Books, New York, New York, 1999, 330 pages.**

This is a challenging and thought-provoking look at ten principles for maintaining a healthy outlook on money, with particular emphasis on the importance of sound financial management in creating a successful family life. The key principles identified include vision, accountability, intensity, diligence, and giving. If you find yourself having difficulty sustaining your momentum in properly managing your finances, this book is full of motivational thoughts to help you maintain your hope.

Ramsey, Dave, *The Total Money Makeover,* **Thomas Nelson, Nashville, Tennessee, 2003, 240 pages.**

If you are experiencing major – or even minor – financial difficulties, you should read this book. It presents Ramsey's comprehensive approach to achieving financial peace, as popularized by his Financial Peace University and his live events. Ramsey believes that personal finance is eighty percent behavioral, so this book is written from that perspective. The dozens of case histories from Ramsey's clients, in their own words, are fascinating reading. Worksheets are included for budgeting, saving, and systematic debt reduction.

Appendix 3

Getting started

My aim in this book has been to learn and share what Solomon tells us about using wealth as God would want us to. I hope this is more than just an intellectual exercise, and that it will help motivate us to take action to manage our financial assets from a Biblical perspective. In this appendix, I have listed some steps that I would recommend as a road map to move in the right direction. Most of the steps below have been mentioned previously in the book – often at some length. Although I think the order in which I have listed them is a logical one, the sequence of the steps is – in most cases – not terribly important. Modify this list to meet your own needs, but please don't fail to transform your attitudes and behaviors, as needed!

1. **Pray that God will help you use your possessions more wisely.** Obviously, this step should be repeated on a regular basis, but start right now! Be as specific with these prayers as you can. For example, if you have large debt and feel overwhelmed by it, pray that God would help you see a way out from under it, and give you the courage to stick with it.

2. **Stop borrowing money.** Debt is not the answer to your financial problems. In fact, it is likely to be the cause of them.
3. **List all your debts.** You need to learn to view debt as an enemy to be avoided and/or attacked. Review Proverbs 6:1-5.
4. **Identify the causes of each of your debts.** (See page 73). This should help you learn what attitudes and behaviors you need to change (and pray about).
5. **Develop a detailed plan for eliminating your debt.** The "debt snowball" is one excellent approach for this. (See page 124).
6. **Estimate your (financial) net worth.** You have listed your debts in step 3. Now list all your assets. The fundamental accounting equation says that Net Worth = Total Assets - Total Liabilities. If you are going to be diligent in financial management, you need some sort of "score card" to measure your progress. That is the purpose for calculating net worth. As you eliminate debt and manage your assets more carefully, your net worth will improve, which should give you positive motivation to keep working (just like seeing your weight drop on the scales keeps you motivated to exercise and watch your diet). WARNING: This step is certainly NOT intended to create a sense of pride or self-sufficiency. Also, if you ever find yourself hesitating to share your wealth because of the "negative" effect it will have on your net worth, wake up! You have missed the point! That will be the signal to re-read the passages in chapters 7 and 8 of this book.
7. **Set some financial goals.** If you have debt, you need to have goals for when the debt should be gone. Spreadsheets (if you are so inclined) are great tools for developing and tracking your plans to, for

example, pay your mortgage off early. Be sure to include benevolence in your goals. (See step 8).
8. **Start a "benevolence envelope."** (See page 127). This will enable you to be able to take care of opportunities to share as they arise, and to be more systematic in sharing with others.
9. **Sell (or give away) some things you don't need.** Any money raised from this can be used to help others or to reduce your debt.
10. **Read *The Richest Man in Babylon*.** This book should help to provide motivation to help you learn to control spending, avoid debt, and start saving.
11. **Read *The Total Money Makeover*.** This book will help you develop your detailed plans for eliminating debt and learning to manage your finances more effectively.
12. **Implement a detailed spending plan.** (See pages 121-122). In order to manage your finances effectively, you will need a specific plan for how your money will be used. Use any plan that you can implement successfully and consistently. *If you are married, make sure this is a joint effort!*
13. **Implement a financial control system that works for you.** The envelope system (see page 122) is an effective system for ensuring that you live by your spending plan. If you decide to use the envelope system, start with envelopes for just a few spending categories – perhaps for groceries, eating out, clothes, and entertainment. These are areas where people often get in trouble. Again, use a system that works for you. *If you are married, make sure this is a joint effort!*
14. **Read a Biblically-based financial management book.** I would particularly recommend Ron Blue's *Master Your Money* and Larry Burkett's *'The World's Easiest Guide' to Finances*. These books will help you

with the details of budgeting, as well as other important elements of your financial plan, such as insurance, retirement planning, and investing.
15. **Teach your children how to apply Biblically-based financial management principles.** Most children will NOT pick up these principles through osmosis. They also will probably not learn them in school. You need to teach your children God's plan for finances, just as you should be teaching them God's plans for salvation, marriage, righteous living, etc.
16. **Keep learning.** Get help, as needed, by talking to successful people with scriptural priorities. Keep reading good books like those in Appendix 2. Study all that the Scriptures have to say on these matters.
17. **Keep praying.** Remember Philippians 4:13: "[We] can do all things through Christ, who strengthens [us]."

Notes

Chapter 1: We need Solomon's financial wisdom

[1] Interview with Gary Player, in *PGA Tour Partners' Club Magazine*.

[2] All scripture quotations, unless otherwise noted, are from the New King James Bible.

[3] According to I Kings 10:14-15, Solomon's annual income in gold was 666 talents (plus significant other income). The *International Standard Bible Encyclopedia* says that a Biblical talent of gold is generally believed to have been around 120 pounds in troy weight (with 12 ounces to the troy pound). His annual income in gold, then, consisted of something on the order of 666 x 120 x 12 = 959,040 ounces of gold. As of early 2007, the price of gold was well over $600 per ounce. The amount of gold received annually by Solomon would, therefore, total approximately 959,040 x 600 = $575,424,000.

[4] Dayton, Howard, *Your Money Counts*, Tyndale House Publishers, Carol Stream, Illinois, 1996, page 8.

[5] Ramsey, Dave, *Financial Peace Revisited*, Viking Penguin, New York, New York, 2003, page 9.

[6] Young, Ian, "Debt Facts," http://www.hoffmanbrinker.com/credit-card-debt-statistics.html, accessed on January 30, 2006.

[7] Allied Debt Consolidation, "Credit Card Debt Statistics," http://www.outtadebt.com/credit-cards.html, accessed on January 30, 2006.

[8] Ramsey, Dave, *More Than Enough*, Penguin Books, New York, New York, 1999, page 79.

[9] Hefner, Jonathan, "Financial Woes Interfere in the Workplace," *Credit Union Magazine*, November, 2004.

[10] Allied Debt Consolidation, "Credit Card Debt Statistics," http://www.outtadebt.com/credit-cards.html, accessed on January 30, 2006.

[11] Stinnett, Nick, and Michael O'Donnell, *Good Kids*, Doubleday, New York, 1996, page 62.

[12] Blomberg, Craig L., *Heart, Soul, and Money*, College Press Publishing Company, Joplin, Missouri, 2000, page 8.

[13] Blomberg, Craig L., *Heart, Soul, and Money*, pages 106-107.

Chapter 2: Wealth is a blessing

[1] Ramsey, Dave, *Financial Peace Revisited*, page 20.

Chapter 5: Work diligently

[1] Scott, Steven K., *The Richest Man Who Ever Lived*, Currency/Doubleday, New York, 2006, page 11.

² Burkett, Larry, *Business by the Book*, Expanded Edition, Thomas Nelson Publishers, Nashville, Tennessee, 1990, page 182.

³ Ramsey, Dave, *More Than Enough*, page 186.

⁴ Quoted in Ramsey, *More Than Enough*, page 182.

Chapter 6: Avoid debt

¹ Blue, Ron, *Master Your Money*, Revised Edition, Thomas Nelson Publishers, Nashville, Tennessee, 1997, page 63.

Chapter 7: Help others

¹ Ramsey, Dave, *Dave Ramsey's Financial Peace: The Great Misunderstanding*, The Lampo Group, Brentwood, Tennessee, 2005, digital video disk.

² Blue, Ron, *Master Your Money*, page 209.

Chapter 10: Transform your life

¹ Ramsey, Dave, *The Total Money Makeover*, Thomas Nelson Publishers, Nashville, Tennessee, 2003.

² United States Census Bureau, "Income 2004: Three-Year-Average Median Household Income by State," http://www.census.gov/hhes/www/income/income04/statemhi.html, accessed on April 21, 2006.

[3] CNN/Money.com, "Credit Card Company Write-Offs Set to Hit a Record High, an S&P Report Finds," http://money.cnn.com/2001/12/26/debt/q_credit/index.htm, accessed on April 21, 2006.

[4] AutoChannel.com, "Average Monthly Car Payments Falling as Loan Terms Extend to Record Lengths, According to Edmunds.com," http://www.theautochannel.com/news/2003/11/25/173435.html, accessed on April 21, 2006.

General Index

Accountability, 141
Ants, 63, 97, 135-136
Associates, 49

Bankruptcy, 14, 78
Bargains, 105-106
Behavior, 17, 119-129, 140, 141
Benevolence, 117, 127, 145
Blomberg, Craig, 16, 17, 137
Blow money, 116, 122
Blue, Ron, 77, 86, 128, 138, 145
Bondage, 75
Boredom, 70
Budget, 60, 106, 120-123, 127, 139, 141, 146
Burkett, Larry, 69, 80, 124, 128, 138, 139, 140, 145
Business by the Book, 69, 138

Car payments, 125
Catastrophe, financial, 73, 124, 128
Children, teaching, 66, 70, 108, 127, 146
Clason, George, 137, 139
Communication, 120
Compassion, 90
Contention, 36
Contentment, 12, 33, 132-133
Contracts, 69
Control, financial, 120-123, 127, 145
Co-signing, 12, 77-79

Counsel, 103
Covetousness, 52, 65, 89
Creator, 96
Credit cards, 14, 78, 119, 123, 125
Crime, 48, 49
Crown Financial Ministries, 140

Daniel, prophet, 58
David, king, 95
Dayton, Howard, 140
Debt, 12, 14, 15, 17, 59, 66, 73-86, 116-117, 123-126, 139, 140, 141, 143-145
Debt-Free Living, 80, 139
Debt snowball, 124, 144
Despair, 50
Diligence, 17, 55-71, 85, 97, 105, 108, 119-123, 126, 129, 141
Discipline, financial, 123-124, 126
Dishonesty, 67-69, 71
Diversification, 12, 61, 70, 105
Divorce, 14, 103

Elisha, prophet, 81, 117
Emergency fund, 96, 100, 123-124, 128
Enemy, 87-88
Enjoyment, 22, 26-27, 36, 41, 99, 107, 114, 116, 118, 134

Envelope system, 122-123, 127, 145
Ethics, 12
Extravagance, 59, 113

Faith, 88, 98, 138
Family, 27, 43, 48, 60, 64, 68, 100, 103, 105-107, 114, 115, 120-124, 127, 139
Farmer, 22, 58, 61
Financial management, 12, 60, 73, 83, 97, 103-104, 114, 119-124
Financial Peace Revisited, 19, 140
Financial Peace University, 141
Firstfruits, 15, 21-22, 25, 27, 114, 116
Foolishness, 21, 50, 51, 56, 78
Freedom, 76, 83
Frivolity, 64, 66-67, 70
Fulfillment, 38, 43, 54, 98, 115

Gazelle, 78
Generosity, 85-91
Get-rich-quick schemes, 12, 41, 43, 44, 54
Getz, Gene, 140
Giving, 12, 15, 85-91, 95, 116-117, 126-127, 138, 140-141
Goals, 96, 98, 144
Grace, 88
Greed, 22, 34, 47-50, 51, 53, 54, 65, 73, 83, 88-90, 116, 119, 124, 126

Happiness, 33, 35, 37

Hatred, 36
Heart, Soul, and Money, 16, 137-138
Honesty, 35, 38, 49, 67-69, 140
Honey, 48, 50, 116
Honor, 31, 33
Hospitality, 59
Humility, 23, 47

Immaturity, 73
Inheritance, 12, 25, 27, 32, 50, 97, 114
Insurance, 60, 69, 70, 96, 100, 128, 136, 139, 146
Integrity, 12, 33, 35, 38
Interest, 53, 69, 81, 82, 125-126
Investing, 12, 60, 61, 88, 90, 117, 122, 138-140, 146

James, 91
Jerusalem church, 91
Joseph, 58
Judgment, 95, 97
Justice, 31, 33, 52, 62, 134

Landmarks, 68-69
Laziness, 12, 15, 56, 61-65, 89, 113, 119, 133
Lender, 73-77, 80-81, 85, 88, 123, 126
Loan, 12, 78-79, 82, 87
Loneliness, 50
Love, 83, 87, 138
Luxury, 48, 50, 107

Marriage, 15, 20, 103, 119-120, 145

General Index 153

Master Your Money, 77, 128, 138, 145
Materialism, 15, 22, 39, 40
Misery, 35, 37, 54, 134
Misfortune, 45
Money, 19, 24, 25, 40, 46, 96
More Than Enough, 141
Motives 56

Net worth, financial, 144

Obedience, 88, 96
Offering, 22, 116-118

Parents, 20
Paul, apostle, 27, 61, 63, 91, 95, 103, 113, 127, 132
Peace, financial, 140, 141
Peer pressure, 49
Planning, 12, 17, 27, 60, 73, 83, 86, 96, 97, 116 120, 124, 127, 128, 135
Player, Gary, 11
Pleasure, 67
Poor, 47, 48, 73, 85, 87, 89, 91, 107, 126, 136; abuse of, 12, 34, 41, 51-54, 69, 135
Poverty, 16, 19, 24, 31, 32, 43, 51, 52, 62-64, 66-67, 89, 131-132, 134
Prayer, 108, 143, 146
Pride, 43, 45-47, 51, 54, 95, 133, 144
Priorities, 12, 45, 53, 58, 59, 70, 114, 117, 146
Prodigal son, 32, 50
Providence, 96

Ramsey, Dave, 19, 70, 85, 121, 124, 140, 141
Repentance, 119, 126
Reputation, 34, 35, 38
Responsibilities, 23, 53, 79, 126
Retirement, 60, 136
Rich in Every Way, 140
Richest Man in Babylon, The, 137, 139, 145
Richest Man Who Ever Lived, The, 56
Righteousness, 21, 31, 33, 52, 93, 97
Risk, 12, 70, 96, 127

Salvation, 20, 32, 88
Satisfaction, 43, 44, 67
Saving, 12, 23, 27, 70, 117-118, 122, 141, 145
Scott, Steven, 56
Security, 12, 14, 25, 27, 114
Selfishness, 88, 107, 126
Shame, 31, 32, 64
Sharing, 27, 38, 95, 107, 114, 116-118, 126-127, 134
Slave, 73-77, 123
Solomon, wealth of, 13; wisdom of, 12-13
Sorrow, 24
Soul, 30
Stewardship, 16, 23, 38, 60, 70, 100, 104, 119, 140
Stress, 14, 15, 43, 59, 76
Strife, 36
Surety, 77-79, 83, 127
Sustenance, 25, 27, 114

Taxes, 67, 82, 83, 116, 138
Teaching children, 66, 70, 108, 127, 146
Thankfulness, 23
Time, 58
Total Money Makeover, The, 121, 141, 145
Trust, 17, 20, 22, 27, 54, 60, 70, 87, 93-100, 102-103, 107, 128-129, 138

Unhappiness, 33, 37
Usury, 52, 53

Vanity, 36, 38, 41, 42, 44, 93, 98-99
Voltaire, 71

Waste, 32, 54, 62
Wealth, attitude toward, 23, 28, 29, 35, 38, 40, 94, 111-118, 129, 139; as a blessing, 16, 20, 22, 24, 26-29, 38, 39, 65, 102, 112-114; building, 116-117; dangers of, 12, 16, 17, 20, 28, 39, 53, 116, 132; God's view of, 17, 26, 28, 39, 56, 129
Wife, virtuous, 17, 101-109, 126, 131
Windfall, 12, 50-51, 54, 116-118
Wisdom, 21, 30, 31, 32, 38, 56, 74, 97, 106, 129
Work, 26, 27, 55-71, 127, 140; rewards of, 12, 26, 27, 104

Workaholism, 12, 37-38, 40, 42-43, 54, 114-115
World's Easiest Guide to Finances, The, 128, 145
Worry, 13, 60, 76, 128

Your Money Counts, 140

Scripture Index

Deuteronomy –
15:6	81
23:19-20	81
28:1	80
28:12	80
28:15	80
28:43-44	80

I Kings –
4:29-34	13
10:14-15	147
10:14-29	13

II Kings –
4:1-7	81
4:7	117

I Chronicles –
21:1-8	95

Psalms –
37:21	76, 80
37:25-26	80
72:2-4	52
72:12-14	52
104:14-15	134
127:2	41-42

Proverbs –
1:1-7	30
1:10-19	48-49
3:9	11, 15
3:9-10	21
3:13-18	30
3:27-28	86

Proverbs -
6:1-5	78, 144
6:6-11	62, 97, 128
6:16-17	45
6:16-19	133
8:10-21	31
8:12-14	31
10:2-3	21
10:4-5	55, 64
10:15	24, 96
10:22	19, 24
11:4	97
11:15	77
11:16	33
11:24-26	89
11:28	93, 97
12:9	24
12:11	66
12:24	64
12:27	65
13:4	64
13:7	96, 98
13:8	24
13:11	68
13:18	31-32
13:22	25, 27, 97
13:23	62
13:25	25
14:4	57-58
14:20	48
14:23	66
14:24	21
15:6	21
15:16-17	36
15:27	47

156   Solomon on Wealth

Proverbs -

16:8	29, 33-34
16:11	68-69
16:16	30
16:18	45
16:26	57
17:1	36, 102
17:8	24
17:18	78
18:9	63
18:10-11	94
18:23	46
19:4	48
19:6-7	48
19:10	48, 50
19:17	85, 87-88
20:4	63
20:13	65
20:16	77
21:5	97
21:5-6	68
21:9	36, 102
21:17	67
21:20	21, 23
21:25-26	65, 89
22:1	33, 108
22:2	94, 96
22:4	21
22:7	73, 75
22:9	87
22:16	51
22:22-23	52, 135
22:26-27	77
22:28	68
22:29	56
23:4-5	40, 42
23:10-11	68
23:20-21	67
24:3-4	21
24:27	57, 59

Proverbs -

24:30-34	62
25:16	48, 50, 54, 116, 118
25:21-22	87
27:13	77
27:23	119
27:23-27	57, 60, 97
28:6	33
28:8	52
28:11	46
28:15-16	52
28:19	66
28:20	39, 41, 43
28:22	41, 43
28:27	89
29:3	31-32
29:7	89-90
30:8-9	131-132
30:14	135
30:21-23	133
30:24-28	135
31:4-7	134
31:8-9	136
31:10-11	101
31:10-12	102
31:10-31	x, 17, 101
31:13-19	105
31:20-22	107
31:24	105
31:27	105
31:28-31	108

Ecclesiastes –

2:18-26	99
2:24	26
3:12-13	26
4:6	36-37
4:8	36-37
5:8	44

Scripture Index 157

Ecclesiastes -
5:8-17	41
5:12-13	45
5:18-20	26
5:19	27
6:1-9	42
6:6	45
7:12	24, 96
7:14	94
8:15	26
9:2	32
9:7-9	26
9:10	57, 60
9:11	32
10:18	63
10:19	46
11:1-2	87
11:6	57, 61, 97
12:13	111
12:13-14	95

Isaiah -
3:13-15	34, 51

Amos -
2:6-7	51

Micah -
2:1-2	34
3:2-3	51

Zechariah -
7:9-10	34

Matthew -
6:19-21	94
6:21	130
6:25-34	60
16:26	30
18:30	75

Matthew -
19:16-22	34
25:31-46	91
25:40	88

Luke -
14:28-30	27
15:11-32	32
16:13	40
17:10	88

John -
9:4	61

Acts -
4:34-35	91
20:35	91

Romans -
12:20	88
13:7-8	82-83

Galatians -
6:9-10	91

Ephesians -
4:28	91, 126-127

Philippians -
4:11-13	132
4:13	146

Colossians -
3:22-24	63

II Thessalonians -
3:10	114
3:10-12	27

I Timothy –
5:14	103
6:6-10	33-34
6:10	40
6:17-19	91, 95, 107, 126

Hebrews –
11:24-26	37

James –
1:27	91, 128, 136
2:14-26	88
2:15-16	90

I Peter –
3:1-6	102

I John –
2:15-17	40

About the author

Stan Bullington was born and raised in Athens, Alabama, and was educated at Athens Bible School, Auburn University, and Purdue University. Since 1987, he has been on the faculty at Mississippi State University, where he is Professor of Industrial and Systems Engineering and a member of the Bagley College of Engineering Academy of Distinguished Teachers. Dr. Bullington teaches courses related to engineering management, including engineering economic analysis, and is the author of numerous technical articles. Stan has taught Bible classes for over thirty years. He loves reading, golf, and camping with his family. He lives in Starkville, Mississippi with his wife, Leanne, and their children Amy, Will, Suzanne, and Andrew.

Contact Information

Solomon on Wealth, is available from bookstores and online booksellers. If you are unable to locate our books through these retail outlets, please order directly from us. You can place an order by:

- Calling us at **662-324-9540**.
- Faxing your order to us at **662-323-1387**.
- Visiting us at **www.bullypulpitpress.com**.
- Mailing your order with payment to:
  Bully Pulpit Press
  P.O. Box 1504
  Starkville, MS 39760

Price: $12.95 US per copy.

Sales tax (only in Mississippi): Add 7.0%.

Shipping (in the U.S.): $4.00 for the first book; $2.00 for each additional book.

Also Available

Study Questions: Questions for Bible studies based on *Solomon On Wealth* are available as a **free** download at **www.SolomonOnWealth.com**.

Seminars: Contact Bully Pulpit Press to arrange a seminar or workshop with the author.